The **Politically Incorrect Guide**™ to

THE GREAT DEPRESSION
AND THE NEW DEAL

Praise for

The **Politically Incorrect Guide**™ to

THE GREAT DEPRESSION AND THE NEW DEAL

"A thorough and impressive critique of FDR and the New Deal which should be required reading in all modern U.S. history and economics courses. I highly recommend this insightful book."

—**Burton W. Folsom, Jr.,** Professor of History, Hillsdale College and author of *New Deal or Raw Deal?: How FDR's Economic Legacy Has Damaged America*

"Robert P. Murphy's splendid guide to the Great Depression and the New Deal is a clear, compelling account of an era that even most economists get wrong. Now that many people are clamoring for a rerun of the New Deal, you owe it to yourself to find out what such a sequel would entail. Murphy's book is the best place to begin your quest."

—**Robert Higgs,** Senior Fellow in Political Economy, The Independent Institute

"Today's central planners cower from the truth about the Great Depression and the New Deal like Dracula before a crucifix. Robert Murphy eviscerates the fantasy version of these episodes that is used to justify destructive and idiotic policies today. You almost feel sorry for the propagandists while reading this book. Almost."

–**Thomas E. Woods, Ph.D.,** author of the *New York Times* bestseller *Meltdown: A Free-Market Look at Why the Stock Market Collapsed, the Economy Tanked, and Government Bailouts Will Make Things Worse*

"Dr. Murphy explains in insightful fashion why the conventional wisdom is neither conventional nor wisdom. He is not only a good economist but can turn the reader into a good economist."

—**Gary Wolfram,** William Simon Professor of Economics and Public Policy, Hillsdale College

"Bob Murphy's *Politically Incorrect Guide*™ *to the Great Depression* provides defenders of liberty the intellectual arsenal they need to counter the myth that capitalism caused, and government cured the Great Depression. Read this book and understand why massively increasing government is not change we can believe in."

–**Congressman Ron Paul**

The **Politically Incorrect Guide**™ to

THE GREAT DEPRESSION
AND THE NEW DEAL

Robert P. Murphy

Since 1947
REGNERY
PUBLISHING, INC.
An Eagle Publishing Company • Washington, DC

Cataloging-in-Publication data on file with the Library of Congress

ISBN 978-1-59698-096-9

Published in the United States by
Regnery Publishing, Inc.
One Massachusetts Avenue, NW
Washington, DC 20001
www.regnery.com

Manufactured in the United States of America

10 9 8 7 6 5 4 3 2 1

Books are available in quantity for promotional or premium use. Write to Director of Special Sales, Regnery Publishing, Inc., One Massachusetts Avenue NW, Washington, DC 20001, for information on discounts and terms or call (202) 216-0600.

Distributed to the trade by:
Perseus Distribution
387 Park Avenue South
New York, NY 10016

To Bob Higgs and Burt Folsom,
whose heavy lifting made this book relatively easy.

CONTENTS

Contents

EVERYTHING YOU LEARNED ABOUT THE GREAT DEPRESSION AND NEW DEAL IS WRONG

If you are a typical American, you learned that the 1920s were a period of wildcat speculation, where the little guy was at the mercy of unregulated big businesses. You learned that the excesses of naked capitalism led to a great stock market crash, an horrific economic contraction, and skyrocketing unemployment. You learned that Herbert Hoover did nothing to alleviate the crisis, merely gazing coolly from his White House office as the laissez-faire market economy collapsed upon itself. You learned that the American people demanded government help and voted overwhelmingly for Franklin D. Roosevelt, whose stirring words provided hope and whose revolutionary programs provided recovery. Finally, to the extent your education deviated from the above account, you learned it was World War II, not FDR, that actually pulled the United States out of the Great Depression.

Every single element of this official narrative is utterly false—and any honest researcher who bothered to check his primary sources would have known it. But most historians know nothing about economics, and most economists know little about history (or even about economics, if CNBC is any guide). The D.C. politicians and bureaucrats can always count on plenty of historians and economists who are only too eager to sing the praises of big government—even if the song's verses don't jibe with the facts. But so long as you don't let historical details trip you up, the Great Depression myths make for a great story. They contrast the indifferent "do-nothing" Hoover against the bold and charismatic Roosevelt, even if, well, Hoover spent unprecedented sums on public works to create jobs, and, er, Roosevelt excoriated Hoover's profligacy on the campaign trail. But the change in presidents is just too good a hook for historians to hang their hats on, and gushing Roosevelt biographers have been only too happy to fill their readers' heads with hagiographies of the great man.

This book is a guide to the most important period of American economic history—one that touches our fundamental understandings of how our economy works and what government should do.

This book fact-checks the myths, shows how they're wrong, and will arm you with the truth. It is one of the great untold—or at least under-told—stories of American history. It is also a story that many in the government, the liberal media, and even academia do not want you to know. But it is the truth. You can look it up.

And this book isn't just about history. Right now the federal government and Federal Reserve are expanding their powers in unprecedented ways. The government is granting trillions of dollars in direct handouts and guarantees to the nation's biggest banks and corporations, while the Federal Reserve stands ready to pump tanker loads of money into the credit markets in the name of "stimulating" the economy. We're told "the lessons of the Great Depression" justify this racking up of enormous debt and this massive intervention of the federal government into what was previously known as the private sector.

But the "history" on which the federal government's power grabs are based is simply a myth. This book will show you what really happened, and arm you against the apologists for the federal juggernaut. It was big government—in alliance with some members of big business—that fueled the 1920s stock market boom and made the 1929 crash inevitable. It was even bigger government under Hoover and then FDR that kept tinkering with the market, delaying recovery, and leading us into the worst economic downturn in American history—and it could happen again, if we're guided by myth rather than fact.

The issues in this book are not mere disagreements between conservative and liberal, Republican and Democrat. Things are much more serious than that now. What happened in the 1930s is repeating itself in our times, with a growing chorus calling for a "new New Deal." Only if enough citizens learn the truth in time will America avoid an even greater Great Depression.

Chapter 1

THE CRISIS

The Great Depression is the most important event in American economic history; it drastically shifted American ideas of economics and politics, with the federal government taking a far more intrusive role in our economy than ever before. First Herbert Hoover, and then Franklin Roosevelt's New Deal, unleashed an unprecedented burst of new government programs—all of which, however, failed to lift America out of the worst economic times in our history. How did it all happen? Let's start with the basic history and then we can examine the possible explanations.

The Roaring Twenties

Part of the shock of the Depression was its sharp contrast to the good times that had preceded it. The "Roaring Twenties" were arguably the most prosperous decade in American history. It wasn't merely that people grew richer during the 1920s. It was more than that; people's lives *changed*. Many households, especially in rural areas, received electricity for the first time. This allowed the proliferation of items that nowadays we consider necessities, such as vacuum cleaners, refrigerators, and toasters.

Guess What?

- The standard account of the Great Depression relies on bad history

- The myths of the Great Depression and New Deal support big government

- The New Deal prolonged the Depression

With more and more households owning radios, the first nationwide radio network made its debut in the mid-1920s. The ratio of automobiles to households almost tripled from 1919 to 1929. The growing availability of electricity, as well as the increased mobility of average Americans, gave rise to professional sports as a big business and Hollywood as a glamorous movie capital.[1] The 1920s were a hectic, exciting time, replete with Prohibition bootleggers and freewheeling flappers.

And yet, amidst the dizzying prosperity and illegal partying, there were growing signs that something was fundamentally wrong. An early warning was the Florida real estate bubble that popped in 1925. But even though investors had seen the dangers of a speculative boom—where asset prices rise far beyond their fundamentals, simply because everyone *expects* them to keep rising—they didn't take the lesson to heart. Instead, they licked their wounds and transferred their over-leveraged portfolios into the stock market.

What goes up, often comes crashing down. The authorities at the Federal Reserve became increasingly alarmed over the Wall Street boom, and tried increasingly stronger measures to moderate its appreciation. But by its very nature, a speculative bubble cannot simply taper off to a gentle plateau. Without a constant influx of new investors to push prices ever higher, the speculative buyer loses interest. Thus the demand falls out from underneath the market, leading to a crash. This is what

What a Way to Go!

"The wife of a Long Island broker shot herself in the heart; a utilities executive in Rochester, New York, shut himself in his bathroom and opened a wall jet of illuminating gas; a St. Louis broker swallowed poison; a Philadelphia financier shot himself in his athletic club; a divorcée in Allentown, Pennsylvania, closed the doors and windows of her home and turned on a gas oven. In Milwaukee, one gentleman who took his own life left a note that read, 'My body should go to science, my soul to Andrew W. Mellon, and sympathy to my creditors.'"

—Historian **William K. Klingaman**

1929: The Year of the Great Crash

happened in October 1929. On the worst two days—dubbed Black Monday and Black Tuesday—Wall Street lost almost 13 percent and then almost 12 percent of its overall value, back to back. This was an inconceivable financial bloodletting, which led to real bloodletting as ruined speculators hurled themselves out of skyscraper windows (as well as committing suicide through other, less noteworthy, means).

Never Was So Much Owed By So Many ...

"Under my very window a gentleman cast himself down fifteen storeys and was dashed to pieces, causing a wild commotion and the arrival of the fire brigade."

—**Winston Churchill**, visiting Manhattan, October 30, 1929.

Quoted in William K. Klingaman, 1929: *The Year of the Great Crash* (New York: Harper & Row, 1989), 289.

The Onset of the Great Depression

Although President Hoover, Secretary of the Treasury Andrew Mellon, and other financial authorities assured the public that the economic successes of the 1920s had merely hit a bump in the road, the facts continued to prove otherwise. As the years dragged on, things inexplicably grew worse and worse. The unemployment rate continued its upward march, averaging 8.9 percent in 1930, then almost 16 percent in 1931, then more than 23 percent in 1932, and finally an astounding 25 percent in 1933. No one in government, let alone the poor man on the street, had any idea how to stop the madness. Nothing like this had ever happened before—or since—in the labor market.

Not only was the Great Depression unmatched in its severity, but its *duration* was unprecedented as well. The United States had been wracked with depressions—or "panics" as they had been called—many times before, but they were typically resolved within two years. And yet three years after the stock market crash of 1929, the economy was still in free fall. From 1929 to 1933, annual production fell an astonishing 27 percent, and the unemployment rate broke 28 percent in March 1933.[2]

A good judge of character

"Coolidge respected but disliked Hoover, whom he called 'Wonder Boy,' because he always seemed to want to change things."

—Robert Sobel

Coolidge: An American Enigma (Washington, D.C.: Regnery, 1998), 242.

Besides rampant joblessness, average Americans suffered through banking panics as well. Before the days of the Federal Deposit Insurance Corporation (FDIC), if a bank went belly-up depositors could lose their life savings. Periodically throughout the early 1930s rumors of unhealthy banks led to bank runs—much like the one depicted in the classic film *It's a Wonderful Life*—where spooked depositors rushed to withdraw their money before the bank ran out. Thousands of banks failed, causing depositors to lose some $1.3 billion by 1933.[3]

Yet beyond the losses, the banking panics undermined the very infrastructure of the American financial system. Without a sound network of banks, how could the economy recover? It seemed to many that capitalism itself was unraveling.

Beyond the hopelessness and misery, another aspect of the Great Depression was the smoldering sense of *injustice*, as millions of breadwinners struggled to find a job, *any* job, to support their families. Incredibly, while much of the nation hovered on the brink of starvation, massive quantities of food and livestock were *deliberately destroyed* in order to fatten profits (at the behest of the federal government).

FDR and the New Deal

And then, into the void left by Herbert Hoover's failed policies, entered a charismatic leader who offered hope. In addition, he offered a radical set of new federal programs designed to bring immediate relief, economic recovery, and also long-term reform, to ensure that the disaster of the Great Depression would never be repeated. In the election

Margin Trading Didn't Cause the Great Depression

In a standard history textbook, students learn that one of the causes of the stock market crash of 1929—and hence of the Great Depression itself—was unregulated "margin trading." The theory is that the wildcat market of the 1920s didn't place restrictions on investors, and so they foolishly borrowed money in order to dabble in the stock market. Because they were so leveraged, even a slight fall in stock prices wiped these naïve investors out, leading to a chain reaction of selling when their brokers made "margin calls." According to this conventional account, the wise curbs put in place by FDR with the creation of the Securities and Exchange Commission and other regulatory agencies was necessary to bring sanity to stock trading, and to prevent the irrational capitalist excesses of the 1920s.

The problem with this "explanation" is that it assumes government bureaucrats understand financial markets better than the professionals, and it also assumes that the regulators are more concerned about investors' money than the investors themselves. The banks and other institutions who lent money to margin traders understood there were risks. They knew that if the value of the underlying collateral—the stock itself—should fall quickly, then the lenders would not only lose their promised interest payments but even some of their principal. And when the market crashed in late 1929, that is exactly what happened.

It is true that margin trading amplified the losses, but to blame the practice is akin to blaming electricity or the English language for "allowing" investors to easily make deals and foolishly throw away their money. The real puzzle is this: Why did so many stock speculators make such bad forecasts, and why did so many lenders let these fools gamble with *their* money? One answer is that the Federal Reserve flooded the credit markets with cheap money in 1927, which encouraged what we've learned to call "irrational exuberance." Left to its own devices, a market economy "regulates" stock speculation better than bureaucrats, just as a market economy makes better computers and novels than a government agency could produce.

of 1932, Franklin Delano Roosevelt won by a landslide, garnering 57 percent of the popular vote to Hoover's 40 percent, and winning 42 (of 48) states.

Roosevelt offered the nation a "New Deal," consisting of a flurry of legislation that expanded the role of the federal government in American life. Advised by his "Brain Trust"—intellectuals who were primarily professors from the Columbia and Harvard law schools—Roosevelt embarked on sweeping initiatives from the moment he entered office.

Roosevelt was sworn in on March 4, 1933, and the very next day declared a national "bank holiday," closing down all banks pending government inspection and approval of their soundness. He called the 73rd Congress to session on March 9, which marked the beginning of the celebrated "Hundred Days," a record-breaking outpouring of new legisla-

A Modest Beginning to a Conservative Presidency

Vice President Calvin Coolidge became president when Warren Harding died in August 1923. Coolidge was on a two-week vacation at his father's farm, "helping to get in the hay, swinging a scythe, handling a pitchfork, and driving a two-horse 'hitch.'" The farmhouse had no phone and no electricity. Historian Paul Johnson describes what happened: "The Coolidge family were awakwened by a Post Office messenger pounding on the door. He brought two telegrams: one from Harding's secretary giving official notification of the President's death, the second from the Attorney-General advising Coolidge to qualify immediately for the office by taking the oath. So the oath was copied out and Coolidge's father, being a notary public, administered it, by the light of a kerosene lamp...."

Paul Johnson, *A History of the American People* (New York: Harper Perennial, 1999), 712–13.

tion. This included the Emergency Banking Act (which gave the president broad powers and allowed him to take America off the gold standard), the formation of the Civilian Conservation Corps (CCC), the Federal Emergency Relief Act (FERA), the Agricultural Adjustment Act (AAA), the creation of the Tennessee Valley Authority (TVA), the Federal Securities Act, the National Employment System Act, the Home Owners Refinancing Act, and—on the hundredth day—the National Industrial Recovery Act, which established the Public Works Administration (PWA) and the National Recovery Administration (NRA).

Further in his administration, Roosevelt signed into law other signature features of the New Deal, many of which are still with us. For example, in 1934 the government created the Securities and Exchange Commission (SEC), with the mission of ensuring financial market transparency and sensible curbs on stock speculation; and 1934 also saw the birth of the National Labor Relations Board (NLRB) and the Federal Housing Administration (FHA). In 1935 the Social Security Act was passed, with the goal of providing old-age, survivor, disability, and—at its inception—unemployment insurance at a time when private relief efforts were deemed inadequate to the task.

Despite his undeniable rhetorical gifts and his cozy "fireside chats," FDR did not charm everyone. Many business leaders feared and loathed him, considering the New Deal to be a dangerous lurch towards the collectivism that was sweeping other industrialized nations. Roosevelt also butted heads with the Supreme Court, which in 1935 threw out the National Industrial Recovery Act as an unconstitutional expansion of federal (and in particular executive) power over free commerce in the *Schechter Poultry* case. In another major setback to the New Deal, the Supreme Court threw out the Agricultural Adjustment Act in 1936 in *United States* v. *Butler*, on the grounds that the federal government did not possess the authority to micromanage agricultural production. Incensed at what he considered the Court's interference with the clear will of the American people, in early 1937 Roosevelt famously threatened to "pack the Court," meaning he wanted the authority to appoint more Justices than the traditional nine. Realizing the danger this plan posed to the checks and balances designed by the Founders to restrain the tyranny of the executive branch, many of Roosevelt's allies deserted him. However, at the same time the Supreme Court became much more compliant, and upheld new legislation that replaced the voided components of the original New Deal. In particular, the Court surprised many business owners by upholding the constitutionality of the National Labor Relations Act in April 1937. A month later the Court gave its blessing to the Social Security Act as well, and Roosevelt decided to drop his controversial plan. The spirit of his New Deal survived, and a costly constitutional crisis had been avoided.

Don't Trust an Economist for Investment Advice

"There may be a recession in stock prices, but not anything in the nature of a crash. Dividend returns on stocks are moving higher. This is not due to receding prices for stocks, and will not be hastened by any anticipated crash, the possibility of which I fail to see."

—**Irving Fisher**, two days after the peak of the bull market, 1929

Quoted in Mark Thornton, "The Great Depression: Mises vs. Fisher," *Quarterly Journal of Austrian Economics* (11: 230-241, 2008), 235.

The 1937–38 "Depression Within the Depression"

Despite the grumblings of the businessmen—and the more conservative Justices of the Supreme Court—the economy seemed to respond to FDR's bold measures, at least for a while. Although still abysmal, the unemployment numbers finally began receding almost the moment Roosevelt took office. Other indicators of economic health, such as Gross National Product, also reversed their staggering decline. Although the recovery was sluggish, it looked as if the New Deal was working. Apparently the huge expansion of the federal government—micromanaging business decisions and putting millions of people on make-work projects—was helping.

But then disaster struck in 1938, in what has been called the "depression within the Depression." Economic output collapsed 3 percent from the prior year, and unemployment rates shot back up, averaging 19 percent

Why Did the Stock Market Crash?

The most persuasive explanation for the 1929 stock market crash blames the Federal Reserve. Throughout the 1920s, but particularly in 1927, the Fed pumped artificial credit into the loan market, pushing down interest rates from their free-market level. Lower interest rates exaggerated the feeling of prosperity, and misled businesses and investors.

In a laissez-faire market where money and banking are not disturbed by the government, the interest rate is a price that tells borrowers how much capital citizens have saved and made available to fund projects. But when the Fed adopts an "easy-money" policy by pushing down interest rates, this signal is distorted and the interest rate no longer does its job of channeling the available capital into the most deserving projects. Instead, an unsustainable boom develops, with firms hiring workers and starting production processes that will have to be discontinued once the Fed slows down its injections of new money.

Many economists point to the Fed hikes in interest rates during 1928 and 1929 as the cause of the stock market crash. In a sense this is true, but the deeper point is that the crash was made inevitable by the *bubble* in the stock market fueled by the artificially cheap credit preceding the hikes. In other words, when the Fed stopped pumping in gobs of new money that *pushed up* the stock market, investors came to their senses and asset prices plunged back towards their pre-bubble level.

for the year. In fact, the monthly unemployment figure broke 20 percent in April 1939, leading Roosevelt's Secretary of the Treasury and close confidant Henry Morgenthau to confess in despair:

> We have tried spending money. We are spending more than we have ever spent before and it does not work. And I have just one interest, and if I am wrong ... somebody else can have my job. I want to see this country prosperous. I want to see people get a job. I want to see people get enough to eat. We have never made good on our promises....I say after eight years of this Administration we have just as much unemployment as when we started....And an enormous debt to boot![4]

Freedom Works

"If business can be let alone and assured of reasonable freedom from governmental interference and increased taxes, that will do more than all kinds of legislation to relieve depression. Local governments are justified in spending all the money necessary for the direct relief of distress. But the nation and the states will only increase the difficulties by undertaking to restore confidence through legislation. It will be the part of wisdom to give business a free hand to supply its own remedies."

—Calvin Coolidge

Quoted in *Silent Cal's Almanack: The Homespun Wit and Wisdom of Vermont's Calvin Coolidge*, edited by David Pietrusza (Create Space Books, 2008), 54–5.

Rosie the Riveter: Happy Times Are Here Again

Ironically, the Depression's grim economic statistics did not truly turn around until the full mobilization needed to fight Nazi Germany and Imperial Japan. With the most employable men fighting overseas, there were plenty of jobs to fill on the homefront as America became the "arsenal of democracy." Whereas the '30s had witnessed nomadic families searching for any odd job, even if just to get food, in the early 1940s there was such a shortage of labor that humming factories lured women and the elderly into the workplace. After a brief dislocation in 1946 as industries reverted back to peacetime production, the post-war U.S. economy zoomed into the 1950s as the world's powerhouse. At long last, the tragedy of the Great Depression began to fade as a horrible memory.

Just the Facts, Ma'am? The Need for Interpretation

Scores of books have been written about the Great Depression and also the New Deal, chronicling the personal tragedies and demonstrations of

One Economist Who Got It Right

"I was one of the only ones to predict what was going to happen. In early 1929, when I made this forecast . . . I said that there [would be] no hope of a recovery in Europe until interest rates fell, and interest rates would not fall until the American boom collapses, which I said was likely to happen within the next few months.

What made me expect this, of course, is one of my main theoretical beliefs that you cannot indefinitely maintain an inflationary boom. Such a boom creates all kinds of artificial jobs that might keep going for a fairly long time but sooner or later must collapse. Also, I was convinced that after 1927, when the Federal Reserve made an attempt to stave off a collapse by credit expansion, the boom had become a typically inflationary one."

—**Friedrich Hayek**, 1975 interview

Quoted in Mark Skousen, "Who Predicted the 1929 Crash?" in *The Meaning of Ludwig von Mises: Contributions in Economics, Sociology, Epistemology, and Political Philosophy*, ed. Jeffrey Herbener (Norwell, Massachusetts: Kluwer Academic Publishers, 2003).

heroism during those dark years. Yet economists need to answer a crucial question in order to guide policymakers *today*: Why was the Great Depression so severe and so long? And did the respective policies of Hoover and FDR help or hurt?

The reader will not be shocked to learn that economic historians do not agree. For good or ill, economic historians can't help but color their interpretation of the historical record with their own views of capitalism. Those who glorify Big Government can construct a seemingly plausible account of the Great Depression and New Deal, in which FDR swoops in and saves the day. This has been the dominant version, the one most readers learned in school, and it makes a good story that fits neatly into the chain of events just described. But as economists continue to study the period, they keep

Why Calvin Coolidge Would Have Voted Against Obama

"When depression in business comes we begin to be very conservative in our financial affairs. We save our money and take no chances in its investment. Yet in our political actions we go in the opposite direction. We begin to support radical measures and cast our votes for those who advance the most reckless proposals.

"This is a curious and illogical reaction. When times are good we might take a chance on a radical government. But when we are financially weakened we need the soundest and wisest of men and measures."

—**Calvin Coolidge**

Quoted in *Silent Cal's Almanack: The Homespun Wit and Wisdom of Vermont's Calvin Coolidge*, edited by David Pietrusza (Create Space Books, 2008), 54.

digging up hard data that glaringly contradicts the official view. More and more economists and historians are beginning to realize that the corrupt politicians who manage to waste our money today were not wizards of efficiency in the 1930s. Some things remain the same: politicians and bureaucrats have always been incompetent and venal when they've chosen to intervene in the economy. That's an economic fact of life.

Books You're Not Supposed to Read

Great Myths of the Great Depression, Lawrence Reed (Midland, MI: Mackinac Center for Public Policy, 2008).

The Causes of the Economic Crisis and Other Essays Before and After the Great Depression, Ludwig von Mises (Auburn, AL: The Ludwig von Mises Institute, 2006)

The Great Depression, Lionel Robbins (Auburn, AL: The Ludwig von Mises Institute, 2007 [1934])

The Reason Why

There are three basic explanations for what happened in the Great Depression.

Explanation #1: The wildcat free market caused the Great Depression, and the New Deal pulled us out of it.

This is the official view, and the one most Americans reflexively believe. It is trumpeted by President Barack Obama—when touting the need for his "stimulus" recovery plan—and has been pounded home over the years by Nobel Prize-winning economist Paul Krugman in his very popular *New York Times* column and blog. It relies on the economic worldview of John Maynard Keynes, and the notion of "aggregate demand." In this interpretation, the inherent excesses of naked capitalism allowed the stock market boom and then crash in 1929. Businesses laid off workers, who then stopped buying products, in a vicious downward spiral. Herbert Hoover did not intervene in this short-circuiting market, because he respected the Constitution and did not believe the federal government should provide direct relief to the unemployed. In fact, they say, Hoover's devotion to a balanced budget led him to raise taxes in 1932, when the economy was already very vulnerable. FDR's New Deal started the road to recovery, but it was ultimately the massive deficit spending of the war years that rescued America's economy from the Depression.

Naturally, those who subscribe to the Keynesian explanation of the Depression favor a huge government stimulus package to "jump start" the economy out of its current woes.

Explanation #2: A market economy goes through natural ups and downs, but the Federal Reserve let the money supply collapse in the early 1930s, turning a normal downturn into the Great Depression.

This view was popularized by Milton Friedman and Anna Schwartz in their classic work, *A Monetary History of the United States*. Many modern-day fans of the free market subscribe to it, because it places the blame for the Depression squarely on the shoulders of incompetent bureaucrats. The most important proponent for this explanation today is none other than Federal Reserve chairman Ben Bernanke. In his earlier life, Bernanke was an academic economist at Princeton. His specialty—ironically enough—was the Great Depression. Today, those who endorse the Friedmanite "monetarist" explanation of the Depression think that the Federal Reserve has responded to our current housing and financial crisis properly by cutting interest rates down to virtually zero percent. These analysts remind everyone that there are "lags" in monetary policy, and that the Fed still has plenty of "ammunition" with which to stimulate the economy.

Coolidge on Hoover

"That man has given me nothing but advice, and all of it bad."

Quoted in Robert Sobel, *Coolidge: An American Enigma* (Washington, D.C.: Regnery, 1998), 242.

The Gold Standard Didn't Cause the Great Depression

Another typical explanation for the Great Depression blames the "obsolete" gold standard. According to this theory, in the early 1930s the industrialized economies were swept by a wave of panic, with depositors withdrawing their funds from the banking system as they hunkered down. In such an environment—so the conventional thinking tells us—the proper move for central bankers was to flood their economies with newly printed money, to offset the hoarding and prevent prices from falling. But unfortunately, the central bankers had their hands tied by the gold standard, and they couldn't implement the right medicine for fear of having their gold reserves flow out of the country.

Blaming the Great Depression on the gold standard makes no sense at all. After all, the classical gold standard had been in place among the major economies for many decades up until World War I, and it had provided a truly golden era of smooth international trade. It was only when the belligerents (except the United States) abandoned gold during the World War that great imbalances in world trade began. Further, the stock market boom and crash itself was directly tied to the Federal Reserve's 1927 decision to bail out the Bank of England. The Fed ignored the rules of the gold standard and inflated the supply of dollars rather than demand that the British government, which had set its exchange rate too high, devalue the pound or encourage price deflation by contracting its own money supply. Rather than deal with the festering dislocations caused by British wartime inflation, the Fed allowed the Bank of England to postpone the day of reckoning. The Fed's burst of new dollars "solved" the immediate crisis—it stopped the drain on Britain's gold reserves—but it also set in motion the Wall Street stock market boom. Like any quick fix that ignores the fundamental problem, the Fed's decision to bail out the Bank of England in 1927 only led to worse problems a few years later.

The gold standard, when obeyed, had the great virtue of keeping currencies stable. It was only *after* governments had abandoned their ties to gold—so that they could print money to pay for World War I—that the world economy became unhinged. The very instability of the early 1930s that allegedly required massive infusions of new paper money would not have existed had the major countries remained tied to gold all along.

Explanation #3: The Federal Reserve fueled the stock market boom of the 1920s with its easy-money policies. After the crash, the Fed did the wrong thing by cutting rates and propping up unsound institutions. Hoover and FDR's interventions in the economy only made things worse.

This third explanation today is most notably associated with former Republican presidential candidate and Texas Congressman Ron Paul, and with investment manager Peter Schiff. Their thinking is based on the business cycle theory of the so-called Austrian school of economics, whose most famous member is 1974 Nobel laureate Friedrich Hayek. According to this explanation, the free market is even more robust and dependable than the Friedmanites give it credit for. The boom-bust cycle is not a natural feature of capitalism, but rather is caused by the Federal Reserve's manipulation of interest rates. In this interpretation, what made the Great Depression so terrible was *not* the falling money supply of the early 1930s, but instead the *injection* of money into the credit markets during the boom of the late 1920s. Moreover, the extraordinary meddling with wage rates by Hoover and then FDR prevented workers from moving to more sensible niches in the economy, thus guaranteeing a decade of massive unemployment.

The proponents of the third explanation argue that today's crisis was caused by Alan Greenspan's low-interest rate policy in the mid-2000s. This fueled the housing bubble, which inevitably popped, causing enormous

The Legend of Silent Cal

Coolidge, it was said, could be "silent in five languages." According to one story, a woman told Coolidge she had bet a friend she could get him to say at least three words. Coolidge replied, "You lose." When Dorothy Parker heard that Coolidge had just died (in January 1933), she said, "How could they tell?"

Quoted in *Silent Cal's Almanack: The Homespun Wit and Wisdom of Vermont's Calvin Coolidge*, edited by David Pietrusza, (Create Space Books, 2008), 23 and 28.

losses to investors. The Bush Administration compounded the problem by propping up the failed institutions, and the new Obama Administration threatens to do even more damage.

If a Policy Failed in the 1930s, Why Would It Work Today?

Supporters of the first and second explanations are familiar with the basic historical facts, though they often sweep the most inconvenient ones under the rug. Keynesians, for example, realize that the federal government tried massive deficit spending during the 1930s, and yet this policy went hand-in-hand with chronic double-digit unemployment. Followers of Friedman, for their part, do not deny that the Federal

Sounds Like Where We Are Now

"We may say that it [the Great Depression] was the result of greed and selfishness. But what body is to be specifically charged with that? Were the wage earners too greedy in getting all they could for their work? Were the managers of enterprise, big and little, too greedy in trying to operate at a profit? Were the farmers too greedy in their efforts to make more money by tilling more land and enlarging their production?

"The most we can say is that there has been a general lack of judgment so widespread as to involve practically the whole country. We have learned that we were not so big as we thought we were. We shall have to keep nearer the ground. We shall not feel so elated, but shall be much safer."

—**Calvin Coolidge**

Quoted in *Silent Cal's Almanack*, 54.

Reserve slashed its rates immediately after the stock market crash, and in fact brought them to record lows in the following years, trying to stimulate the economy through monetary policy.

So why then do today's Keynesians (such as Paul Krugman) and today's Friedmanites (such as Ben Bernanke) recommend what appear to be *the exact same policies* as a cure for our present financial crisis? If their prescribed medicines led to disaster the *last* time they were implemented, why in the world should we favor huge deficits or easy-money policies today?

The 1920s: Roaring Prosperity or Unsustainable Boom?

Depending on one's ideological preconceptions, the "Roaring '20s" were either a glorious success of relatively laissez-faire principles, or they showed the inherent instability of a pure capitalist economy. The fan of the free market triumphantly points to the amazing economic growth of the 1920s, and attributes it to the conservative fiscal policies engineered by Secretary of the Treasury Andrew Mellon and President Calvin Coolidge. In 1921 the top income tax bracket was a shocking 73 percent, but Mellon reduced it to 25 percent by 1925. Mellon also cut taxes for the poor, with the lowest bracket falling from 4 to 1.5 percent in the same period. Perhaps most impressive of all, Mellon was able to slash tax rates while running federal budget surpluses *every year* of the Coolidge presidency.

The critic of the free market, on the other hand, tries to dismiss the apparent "prosperity" of the 1920s as a house of cards. To such a cynic, the laissez-faire policies of Calvin Coolidge were a prelude to disaster, as evidenced by the crash of 1929 and the following decade of Depression.

The true story is more nuanced, and draws from both of these extremes. Much of the prosperity of the 1920s was real; households really did acquire cars, electricity, and appliances such as vacuum cleaners and toasters. The standard of living for the average American really did rise

The Keynesians and Friedmanites respond that *things would have been even worse* in the 1930s if their solutions hadn't been implemented. In other words, they claim that things were so bad, that even the new remedies were not enough to bring quick relief.

But the problem with this rhetorical dodge is that it ignores history and the fact that America's free market economy had always rebounded from its previous depressions—usually within two years and at most within five—with far less pain (and much less government intervention) before

at an impressive rate throughout the decade. Much of this success can indeed be credited to Mellon's conservative fiscal policies.

However, at the same time, there were forces coming *not* from the free market, but from government intervention, that disturbed this legitimate economic growth. The Federal Reserve flooded the credit markets with cheap money, and it especially opened up the dollar spigot in 1927 (in an effort to ease the gold outflows from the Bank of England). Superimposed on the productive expansion of the United States economy, then, was an *unsustainable boom* fueled by the Fed's inflation, particularly in the last few years of the decade. When the Fed became concerned and tried to put on the brakes, the stock market faltered and eventually crashed.

The fans of the free market are correct to blame the government, not capitalism, for the stock market crash and the ensuing Great Depression. However, many of these writers think that everything was going fine into 1929, and that boneheaded government blunders at the last moment ruined a perfectly healthy stock market. The reality is that Andrew Mellon and Calvin Coolidge, though they implemented excellent tax and spending policies, did *not* understand the pernicious influence of the Federal Reserve. The leftist critics of capitalism are therefore correct when they label the stock market boom as unsustainable, but these critics fail to see that the blame lies with government intervention into the banking and monetary system.

the 1930s. How is it that policies that coincided with the most shocking collapse and most sluggish recovery can ever be recommended? Well, for Keynesians, the answer is simple: it gives the government more power and authority, and there are plenty who applaud such statist measures for their own sake, believing that government manipulation of the economy can make it more "rational" or "just" or better direct its resources (that is, direct them where politicians or bureaucrats want them to go). And on the surface, it *seemed* as if the massive deficit spending during World War II finally ended the Depression, so a Keynesian true believer wouldn't lose sleep over the failed decade of deficit spending during the 1930s.

Books You're Not Supposed to Read

The Politically Incorrect Guide to American History, Thomas E. Woods Jr. (Washington, D.C.: Regnery, 2004)

The Politically Incorrect Guide to Capitalism, Robert P. Murphy (Washington, D.C.: Regnery, 2007)

Free to Choose, Milton Friedman and Rose Friedman (New York: Harcourt, Inc., 1990)

For their part, the Friedmanites have a much more plausible explanation than the Keynesians. After all, the money supply really did shrink by a third from 1929 to 1933; that certainly seems like it would kick the economy while it was already down. What's more, Friedman's explanation is appealing to those who disapprove of massive government spending, because it allows for a technical fix by the Fed. However, the Friedmanites cannot get around the historical facts: there was nothing unprecedented about the speed of the collapse in the money supply, or in the price deflation, of the early 1930s. If Friedman is right that the Federal Reserve's *inaction* caused the Great Depression, then why didn't the U.S. experience even worse catastrophes before 1913, when the Fed didn't even *exist*?

We know that there were no such catastrophes. Before the creation of the Fed, and back in the days when the federal government took no active role in fighting economic downturns, somehow depressions always managed to sort themselves out fairly quickly. It was only when both the federal government and the Federal Reserve rolled up their sleeves to really *fight* a downturn that America suffered through the worst economic crisis in its history. As we will see, economic theory, historical fact, and common sense all lead to the same conclusion: the government caused the Great Depression, the New Deal prolonged the misery, and World War II hurt the private sector even more.

Chapter 2

BIG-GOVERNMENT HERBERT HOOVER MAKES THE DEPRESSION GREAT

In order for the deification of FDR and his New Deal to make any sense, it is necessary to cast Herbert Hoover as a "do-nothing" reactionary, hiding behind the Constitution while the people suffered. Yet nothing could be further from the truth. As Hoover explains in his memoirs:

> With the October-November stock-market crash the primary question at once arose as to whether the President and the Federal government should undertake to mitigate and remedy the evils stemming from it. No President before had ever believed there was a governmental responsibility in such cases. No matter what the urging on previous occasions, Presidents steadfastly had maintained that the Federal government was apart from such eruptions; they had always been left to blow themselves out. Presidents Van Buren, Grant, Cleveland and Theodore Roosevelt had all remained aloof....
>
> Because of this lack of governmental experience, therefore, we had to pioneer a new field. As a matter of fact there was little economic knowledge to guide us.[1]

Guess What?

◆ Herbert Hoover didn't believe in laissez-faire

◆ Hoover's big-government policies created the Great Depression

◆ Many of the "revolutionary" policies of the New Deal were in fact inaugurated under Hoover

It is ironic that Hoover believed the above passage provided evidence for his *innocence* in the matter. It's rather as if a doctor dismissed a remedy that always worked—letting time heal economic wounds—in favor of massive drug intervention, never before tried. Not only did these drugs not work, they made the patient sicker than he'd ever been in his life. But Hoover did not come to the logical conclusion that he had made a mistake. Instead, he simply took it for granted that the failure of his new remedies only proved how bad the situation must have been; it was inconceivable to him that his policies *made* the situation so bad. Hoover's unshakeable conviction in the need for activist government—even after having decades to reflect on the subject—is evident in his *Memoirs* and how he treats Andrew Mellon:

> [After the stock market crash, two] schools of thought quickly developed within our administration discussions.
>
> First was the "leave it alone liquidationists" headed by Secretary of the Treasury Mellon, who felt that government must keep its hands off and let the slump liquidate itself. Mr. Mellon had only one formula: "Liquidate labor, liquidate stocks, liquidate the farmers, liquidate real estate." He insisted that, when the people get an inflation brainstorm, the only way to get it out of their blood is to let it collapse.... He said: "It will purge the rottenness out of the system. High costs of living and high living will come down. People will work harder, live a more moral life. Values will be adjusted, and enterprising people will pick up the wrecks from less competent people."...
>
> At great length, Mr. Mellon recounted to me his recollection of the great depression of the seventies which followed the Civil War.... He told of the tens of thousands of farms that had been foreclosed; of railroads that had almost wholly gone into the hands of receivers; of the few banks that had come through

unscathed; of many men who were jobless and mobs that roamed the streets. He told me that his father had gone to England during that time and had cut short his visit when he received word that the orders for steel were pouring toward the closed furnaces; by the time he got back, confidence was growing on every hand; suddenly the panic had ended, and in twelve months the whole system was again working at full speed.[2]

Note here the strength of Mellon's position. He didn't cherry pick his anecdotes by focusing on a mild downturn. On the contrary, he was recalling what had been, at that time, the longest depression in U.S. history. (According to the National Bureau of Economic Research, the contraction officially lasted from the third quarter of 1873 through the first

The Buck Doesn't Stop Here

In his memoirs, Hoover asserted that the "Great Depression did not start in the United States.... Our domestic difficulties standing alone would have produced no more than the usual type of economic readjustment which had re-occurred at intervals in our history." So what caused the depression? "By early 1931, we were convalescing from our own ills when an economic hurricane struck us from abroad. The whole financial and economic structure of Europe collapsed at this time as a result of the delayed consequences of the First World War, the Versailles Treaty, and internal policies."

Herbert Hoover, *The Memoirs of Herbert Hoover: The Great Depression, 1929-1941* (New York: The Macmillan Company, 1952), vi.

quarter of 1879, about five and a half years.[3]) Even so, the "liquidation-ist" medicine eventually worked, and recovery kicked in apparently much faster than many observers had expected. Inasmuch as the 1930s depression turned out far worse—and lasted for twice as long[4]—after Hoover *rejected* Mellon's advice, one might think Hoover, in retrospect, would have given more credence to Mellon's counsel. But immediately following the passage above Hoover writes:

> I, of course, reminded the Secretary that back in the seventies an untold amount of suffering did take place which might have been prevented; that our economy had been far simpler sixty years ago, when we were 75 per cent an agricultural people contrasted with 30 per cent now; that unemployment during the earlier crisis had been mitigated by the return of large numbers of the unemployed to relatives on the farm; and that farm economy itself had been largely self-contained. But he shook his head with the observation that human nature had not changed in sixty years.
>
> Secretary Mellon was not hard-hearted....He felt there would be less suffering if his course were pursued. The real trouble with him was that he insisted that this was just an ordinary boom-slump....[5]

Secretary Mellon was right: had Hoover followed the practice of his predecessors, we would not remember him today as presiding over the worst economic calamity in U.S. history. (Quick! Who was president during the depression of the 1870s when Mellon's strategy was heeded?) And though we can quibble about the word "ordinary," Mellon was also correct in saying that the depression would have been a boom-slump, comparable to all earlier ones, if only Hoover's administration had pursued the same laissez-faire approach that all earlier administrations had followed.

The stock market and economy in general were already deep into an unsustainable boom when Herbert Hoover took office. In that sense, a bust and the ensuing small "d" depression were unavoidable, no matter what Hoover did in office. But Hoover tried to fight the depression with policies so destructive that, in retrospect, one almost wonders if he were a Soviet agent sent to undermine the American economy.

On one point at least, the liberal historians are partly right. Herbert Hoover made the depression of the 1930s great—but he did so by following the very policies they support. Hoover's policies created the Great Depression precisely because he *abandoned* the laissez-faire approach that he himself acknowledged all earlier presidents had followed when faced with similar circumstances.

Herbert Hoover: Consistent Critic of Capitalism

The skeptical reader can rest assured that Hoover's claims to have rejected Mellon's "liquidationist" advice were not merely self-serving lies penned in his diary after the fact. On the contrary, Herbert Hoover was a consistent critic of unfettered capitalism throughout his career in the government, even during the Roaring '20s when the (relatively) free market was working wonders. His documented actions of the time, as well as the reports of contemporaries—including labor leaders—prove that Herbert Hoover was not the free market ideologue people think he was. In fact, he often butted heads with his boss, Calvin Coolidge, who was a far better (though still impure) exemplar of the "small government fanatic" whom leftists love to ridicule. (We note in passing that laissez-faire Coolidge presided over a booming economy, while activist Hoover's economic record was decidedly subpar.)

Our brief chronicle of the early Hoover begins in 1919, when he was appointed by (Democratic) President Wilson to direct a conference on labor-management relations. The conference ultimately issued many "progressive" recommendations, including an expansion of collective bargaining, a reduction in work hours, the abolition of child labor, and national old-age insurance. Hoover himself endorsed these recommendations, and noted that the "extreme right" (composed of groups such as the Boston Chamber of Commerce) opposed the ideas.

In 1921 (Republican) President Harding appointed Hoover as Secretary of Commerce. During the postwar depression of 1920–1921, Hoover "set out to reconstruct America" (his words) and urged Harding to establish the President's Conference on Unemployment. Looking back on not just this conference but earlier efforts, Hoover wrote:

> We developed cooperation between the federal, state, and municipal governments to increase public works. We persuaded employers to "divide" time among their employees so that as many as possible would have some incomes. We organized the industries to undertake renovation, repair, and, where possible, expand construction.[6]

Throughout 1921, Hoover did what he could to persuade Congress to enact public works programs to stabilize the economy. Fortunately, the depression ended before Hoover's grandiose plans could be realized. (His prescriptions would have to wait until his own presidential administration to show their potency.) Other notable "accomplishments" included Hoover's successful campaign against U.S. Steel, winning a reduction from 12- to 8-hour workdays in 1923, and his role in the 1926 passage of the Railway Labor Act, which Murray Rothbard describes as "America's first permanent incursion of the Federal government into labor-management relations."[7]

Hoover's "New Economics"

To make sense both of Hoover's presidential actions and his (much later) recollections of the Great Depression, we need to understand the economic worldview that guided him. Hoover had been converted to a supposedly enlightened "new economics" that he believed would prevent the needless suffering that had typified all earlier depressions. As Hoover explained in a speech on May 12, 1926:

> [N]ot so many years ago—the employer considered it was in his interest to use the opportunities of unemployment and immigration to lower wages irrespective of other considerations. The lowest wages and longest hours were then conceived as the means to obtain lowest production costs and largest profits.... But we are a long way on the road to new conceptions. The very essence of great production is high wages and low prices, because it depends upon a widening... consumption, only to be obtained from the purchasing-power of high real wages and increased standards of living.[8]

Hoover's words are remarkably "modern," and in fact anticipated the allegedly revolutionary Keynesian analysis that would sweep the world a decade later. Hoover's view reflected the popular misconception that cyclical downturns were the result of "overproduction" and "underconsumption." In short, if business got ahead of itself and produced too much stuff, and at the same time kept its prices too high and/or paid its workers too little, then it was clearly impossible for the community as a whole to *afford* all of the product. Sales would fall off, inventory would accumulate, and the businesses would need to do something.

Now here is where the "new economics" came into play. Left to their own self-seeking devices, businesses would respond to a downturn by slashing the prices they charged, yes, but *also* by slashing costs, through cutting wages and/or laying workers off. But ironically, so Hoover and his fellow underconsumptionists believed, trying to pin the belt-tightening on the workers was self-defeating. An individual firm might enhance its bottom line by cutting its wage payments more than its prices. But if *all* firms try to employ this strategy at the same time, Hoover thought, then they will clearly fail, because it is after all the workers who use their paychecks to pay for the products these businesses were trying to sell. In other words, by slashing wages, firms were undercutting their own collective customer base and the demand for each other's products. In the famous rule favored by Henry Ford and other "enlightened" businessmen at the time: "You have to pay the worker enough to buy back the product."

Given Hoover's diagnosis of the sickness, his cure for an economic downturn makes perfect sense. If workers aren't earning enough to buy all the products generated by businesses, then the obvious remedies are to boost workers' buying power and restrict production. As president, Hoover's policies achieved precisely these goals. He successfully urged businesses to keep wage rates constant even while they were forced to cut their prices—meaning that workers' paychecks would go further and buy more products—and his signing of the infamous Smoot-Hawley tariff (1930) was based on his desire to support farmers' incomes. Hoover's long-standing support for public works projects during a depression is also understandable as a means to prevent incomes from collapsing precisely when businesses are suffering from a fall in demand for their products.

True to his theory, Hoover not only wanted to bolster consumption, but he also sought to "close the gap" by restricting production. As president, Hoover ordered a massive increase in the deportations of immigrants. He supported spread-the-work schemes, whereby struggling businesses wouldn't lay off the most inefficient workers, but would rather maintain staff levels with shortened workweeks. He even attributed partial blame for the hard times on the introduction of "labor-saving devices,"[9] appealing to the Luddite fallacy that new machines are a curse because they throw people out of work. In light of his writings as well as his policies, Hoover clearly thought there was a fixed amount of work to be done in the economy, and he further believed that this delicate balance could be upset if the more capable employees worked too long, or if new immigrants and new machines "took jobs" from everyone else.

Though understandable—they infect our political leaders and financial pundits to this very day—Hoover's theories were completely fallacious. High wages do not *cause* prosperity, they are rather an *indication* of prosperity. Ultimately, it doesn't matter how many green pieces of paper employers hand out to workers. Unless workers have first *physically produced* the goods (and services), there will be nothing on the store shelves for them to buy when they attempt to spend their fat paychecks.

Hoover was correct in his 1926 speech to note that American workers enjoyed both higher "real wages" (meaning money-wages compared to the cost of living) and a higher standard of living than workers in other countries. But American workers were paid more by their employers because they *produced* more. No matter how "enlightened" business leaders in Mexico were, they could not possibly have given their employees the same purchasing power as their counterparts to the north. This is because, on average, Mexican workers were not as productive, and so in their role as consumers it was a physical impossibility that they could acquire the same amount of goods per capita as Americans. If more stuff is produced within America than within Mexico, obviously Americans are going to have a higher standard of living, regardless of "wages policy."

The simple formula of paying the workers "enough to buy back the product" overlooks the fact that there are people *other than employees* who make up the economy. Most obvious are the entrepreneurs and shareholders who own the businesses that employ "the workers." But there are also the owners of all resources besides labor. The workers at an automobile plant don't crank out thousands of cars with their bare hands. Rather, their raw labor is augmented (and tremendously so) by the building site, steel, rubber, tools, and assembly line contributed by other people, and by the organizational talent of the manager overseeing the operation. If the auto workers received total wages equal to the total prices of all the cars that passed through their hands, then the firm in question would have no money left over to pay its suppliers. But this in turn would mean no demand for the products of the tire producers, and hence no way for the tire manufacturer to pay *his* workers.

Even on its own terms, Hoover's philosophy of high wages to support "purchasing power" makes no sense. It fails at the first step in the argument: If hard times hit and cause an employer to ask his twenty employees to accept a pay cut of $10 per week, this doesn't mean $200 worth of "demand" has suddenly disappeared from the system. The reduction in total weekly paychecks is exactly counterbalanced by the employer's earnings, which are now $200 higher than they would have been without the pay cut. (Of course, even with the pay cut, the business's earnings would be lower in a depression than they were during the boom period, but we are here looking at the impact of the wage cut per se.) Hoover was quite simply wrong when he said that cutting wages would reduce the demand for products in general; Hoover missed the fact that wage cuts give employers the means to increase *their* spending (either on personal consumption or to invest). It might strike some as unfair that workers should have to shoulder any of the pain during a depression, but it is patently false to argue that wage cuts reduce the total amount of income available to buy products.

Ironically, Hoover was fully aware that propping up wage rates (amidst falling sales) would mean that *other people* had to take the hit. In the presidential campaign of 1932 Hoover boasted of his record: "For the first time in the history of depression, dividends, profits, and the cost of living have been reduced before wages have suffered."[10] Yet Hoover did not make the obvious connection that falling dividends and profits would reduce the "purchasing power" of shareholders. To reiterate our point: One might say that it's nicer or fairer for the fat cats to suffer the full loss during a downturn, but it is simply not true to argue that shielding wages in this way somehow preserves the total demand for products. Urging employers to give gifts to their employees doesn't make the community richer as a whole, because the gain to the workers is perfectly balanced by the loss to the employers.

Beyond the non sequitur upon which it was based, Hoover's theory overlooked the *purpose* of falling prices and wages during a depression. The boom period of the 1920s was partly illusory. The Federal Reserve kept interest rates artificially low by creating money out of thin air and pumping it into the credit markets. Businesses were misled by the false price signals, and began more long-term projects than could be "funded" by the amount of real savings in the economy. In a word, the structure of the U.S. (and world) economic system by 1929 was *unsustainable*.

By focusing on aggregate monetary conditions such as "total wage payments," Hoover completely overlooked the fact that real, physical resources had to be rearranged in order to correct the imbalances in the economy. It wasn't that "business" was producing too much, but rather that some sectors were producing too much, while other sectors were producing too little, in light of the economy's supplies of resources, the skills and desires of its workers, and the tastes of its consumers.

He Should Have Stuck to Making Cars

"Nearly everything in this country is too high priced. The only thing that should be high priced in this country is the man that works. Wages must not come down, they must not even stay on their present level; they must go up."

—**Henry Ford**, following a White House conference, November 1929.

Quoted in Richard K. Vedder and Lowell E. Gallaway, *Out of Work: Unemployment and Government in Twentieth-Century America* (New York: New York University Press, 1997), 92.

The only way to rectify the situation—to transform the economy into a sustainable configuration—was to shuffle workers and resources. Some enterprises had to be shut down immediately, releasing their workers and freeing up the raw materials they would have consumed had they

Labor Unions Heart Hoover

"The President's conference has given industrial leaders a new sense of their responsibilities.... Never before have they been called upon to act together... [I]n earlier recessions they have acted individually to protect their own interests and... have intensified depressions."

—Editorial in the *American Federationist*, January 1, 1930, a labor union publication touting how Hoover was different from bad old laissez-faire presidents of the past

Quoted in Murray N. Rothbard, *America's Great Depression*, Fifth Edition (U.S.A.: The Ludwig von Mises Institute, 2008), 213–14.

remained in business. Now in a socialist command economy, if the dictator suddenly decides he no longer likes the old plan, he can simply draw up a new one, and then order the comrades at the closed factories to relocate to the expanding ones. There is no period of "unemployment" when everyone serves at the whim of the dictator.

But in a market economy, workers are free to choose their occupations, and the owners of raw materials can sell their property to whomever they desire. Yet with this freedom comes the unfortunate necessity of prolonged spells of unemployment and "idle resources," when the workers and raw materials are searching for a new home in the complex economy. In a free market, prices guide everyone towards the configuration where each participant can best contribute and also reap the most benefits from the division of labor. The industries that need to expand are the ones that can afford to keep their wages up, and so they attract workers. The industries that need to contract are the ones hit hardest by the fall in demand, and so they have to slash prices and wages the most, thereby driving workers away.

Herbert Hoover thought it would help workers to tell employers to prop up wage rates during a depression. He was wrong. The artificially high wages simply ensured that the laid-off workers—those who had been associated with unsustainable enterprises in 1929—could not re-enter the productive side of the economy. Instead they remained in a growing pool of idle labor, priced too high for employers to afford. Hoover's high-wage policy was the first of several measures he undertook to unwittingly spawn the Great Depression.

Making the Depression Great, Step 1: Prop up Wages

True to his "new economics," after the stock market crash Hoover quickly convened a series of White House conferences with leading financiers and businessmen, starting on November 18, 1929. He won their agreement to aim for the maintenance of wages, positions, and investment spending. If this proved impossible, the business leaders would cut wages more slowly than product prices (meaning profits would take the hit before the workers), and unavoidable reductions in hours would be spread out among the workers, rather than eliminating positions outright through layoffs. The business leaders not only agreed—Henry Ford even promised to *raise* wages—but also appointed their representatives to a special advisory committee that would coordinate the government-industry response to the crisis. On December 5 Hoover truthfully told a group of industrialists:

> [Your agreement is] an advance in the whole conception of the relationship of businesses to public welfare. You represent the business of the United States, undertaking through your own voluntary action to contribute something very definite to the advancement of stability and progress in our economic life. This is a far cry from the arbitrary and dog-eat-dog attitude of the business world of some thirty or forty years ago.[11]

Hoover would continue this pressure throughout his term. Summarizing his boss's position (whether or not he personally thought it wise), Treasury Secretary Mellon explained in 1931:

In this country, there has been a concerted and determined effort on the part of both government and business not only to prevent any reduction in wages but to keep the maximum number of men employed, and thereby to increase consumption.

It must be remembered that the all-important factor is purchasing power, and purchasing power...is dependent to a great extent on the standard of living...that standard of living must be maintained at all costs.[12]

Economic historians have shown that Hoover and Mellon were not blowing smoke to the voters. What economists call "real wages" actually rose during the early 1930s, because businesses cut money-wages either not at all or very reluctantly, while the prices of most goods and services were plummeting. This perversely made labor relatively more expensive for businesses to hire, and guess what? During a huge economic slump, when the relative price of workers rose (because of Hoover's misguided worldview), businesses hired fewer workers. Economists Richard Vedder and Lowell Gallaway explain:

While the initial increase in unemployment can be largely explained by the productivity shock, the very sharp rise in unemployment in 1931 was not related to further declines in output per worker. Productivity per worker changed little, actually rising somewhat.... Money wages fell, but rather anemically. Whereas in the 1920–1922 depression a roughly 20 percent fall in money wages was observed in one year, the 1931 decline was less than 3 percent. By contrast, prices fell more substantially, 8.8 percent, so real wages actually rose significantly in 1931, and were higher in that year than in 1929, despite lower output per worker. The 1931 price [declines], accompanied by a failure of money wages to adjust...seemed to be the root cause of the rise in unemployment to over 15 percent in 1931.[13]

The comparison with the previous depression of the early 1920s is instructive. Herbert Hoover and his allies in the labor movement thought it unconscionable that labor should have been "liquidated" during that downturn, to use Andrew Mellon's politically incorrect term. Indeed, during that earlier depression it must have seemed unbearable for workers to see their paychecks slashed by 20 percent in a single year (though other prices were falling too, cushioning the blow). Yet when the economy must readjust after an unsustainable boom, the prices of resources—including labor—need to change in order to facilitate the movement of workers to the correct sectors.

We're in the Money—Too Bad You're Out of Work

Here's a shocking statistic: if you managed to keep your job in the Great Depression, your buying power probably went up—and in fact rose faster than it did during the boom times. Herbert Hoover's "high wage policy" was so successful that in the worst economic crisis in American history, real wages went up at a compounded annual rate of three percent for the years 1929 to 1933. That was significantly higher than wages rose during the Roaring '20s. Of course these high wages came at a price: namely high unemployment, as struggling businesses, paying inflated salaries, couldn't afford to employ as many workers. The economists Richard Vedder and Lowell Gallaway conclude that Hoover's high wage policy "is the root cause for the extraordinary increase in unemployment in the years following the stock-market crash."

Richard K. Vedder and Lowell E. Gallaway, *Out of Work*, 82.

He'll Go Down in History, All Right

"There never has been a crisis such as we have had as the stock market crash that threw...millions out of employment that there wasn't a wholesale reduction in wages.... If Hoover accomplishes nothing more in all of his service to the government, that one outstanding thing of his administration—no reduction in wages—will be a credit that will be forever remembered not by the working classes alone but by business men as well, because without money in the pay envelope business is the first to suffer."

—Secretary of Labor **James Davis**, May 1930, on Hoover's unprecedented high-wage policy, which had the unintended effect of producing an unprecedented depression

Richard K. Vedder and Lowell E. Gallaway, *Out of Work*, 93–94.

Things were very bad—briefly—during the earlier depression. The annual unemployment rate peaked at 11.7 percent in 1921, but it had fallen to 6.7 percent by the following year, and was down to an incredible 2.4 percent by 1923.[14] That is how a market with flexible wages and prices quickly corrects itself after a Fed-induced inflationary boom. But because the "compassionate" Hoover forbade businesses from cutting wages after the 1929 crash, unemployment went up and up and up, hitting the unimaginable monthly peak of 28.3 percent in March 1933.[15] For the quarter of the labor force thrown out of work, the fact that "[f]or the first time in the history of depression, dividends, profits, and the cost of living have been reduced before wages have suffered," was little consolation.

Making the Depression Great, Step 2: Cripple International Trade

Even the typical U.S. history textbook lays partial blame for the Depression on the infamous Smoot-Hawley Tariff Act of 1930, which imposed massive tax hikes on Americans who bought imported goods. Throughout the 1920s, Hoover had felt the government needed to help U.S. farmers, who were not sharing in the prosperity as much as other segments of the country. After the stock market crash, prices began falling, including farm prices. True to his purchasing power theory of depressions, Hoover worried that the decline in farm income would exacerbate the crisis. Yet rather than simply *asking* American consumers to pay more for food (the way he asked big business to maintain wages), Hoover left nothing to chance and used the force of government to impose the price hikes. Smoot-Hawley raised taxes on thousands of imported goods to record levels.

It is said that the one issue on which virtually all economists agree is that "protectionist" barriers only serve to make countries poorer. Indeed, more than a thousand economists petitioned Hoover to veto the tariff bill. Part of the disaster of Smoot-Hawley was the trade war it inspired: other countries

Unintended Consequences

"[T]he Smoot-Hawley tariff was a direct attack on our own home economy. . . . We needed imports to help make our own industrial products. A tariff hike, therefore, crippled our own leading industries. The tariff on tungsten, for example, hurt steel; the tariff on linseed oil damaged the paint industry. General Motors and Ford were the premier carmakers of the world, but the Smoot-Hawley tariff increased the duty on over eight hundred items used in making cars. U.S. automakers, then, took a double hit. First, they sold fewer cars because Europeans slapped retaliatory tariffs on the United States. Second, they had to pay higher prices for hundreds of items needed to make cars. No wonder American car sales plummeted from over 5.3 million in 1929 to 1.8 million in 1932."

—Historian **Burt Folsom**

Burton Folsom, Jr., *New Deal or Raw Deal? How FDR's Legacy Has Damaged America* (New York: Threshold Editions, 2008), 31–32.

retaliated by raising tariffs on U.S. goods. The anti-American backlash included European repudiation of debts incurred during World War I.[16]

Yet regardless of how other countries responded, Hoover's decision to strengthen trade barriers made Americans poorer. It is true that a hike in any single tariff helps the American producers of the good in question, by weakening foreign competition in that market. But Americans in general are still hurt, because a new tariff simply raises prices for American consumers trying to buy the good. Moreover, American exporters are hurt

A Foolish Consistency: Barring Foreign Goods and Workers

Consistent with his notion of a fixed number of jobs, Hoover writes in his memoirs, "In order to cope successfully with the unemployment problem, I felt it necessary to restrict immigration." He then presents the following table with pride:

	Immigrants	Emigrants
1929	279,678	69,203
1930	241,700	50,661
1931	97,139	61,882
1932	35,576	103,295

Hoover also (approvingly) contrasts his own record of deportations—peaking at 19,865 in Fiscal Year 1933—with that of FDR, when deportations fell to 8,879 in 1934. It's a strange measure of success to have more people leaving your country than entering it.

Herbert Hoover, *The Memoirs of Herbert Hoover*, 48.

by a tariff protecting a particular U.S. industry, because the extra hurdle to imports means that foreigners have fewer dollars with which to buy American exports. (Total U.S. exports dropped from $7 billion in 1929 to $2.5 billion in 1932,[17] though this fall was partially due to the general economic decline and to price deflation.) Because the U.S. was a net exporter of agricultural products, hiking tariff barriers ironically hurt American farmers more than many other producers.

If every individual were forced to grow his own food, sew his own clothes, and build his own home, it would certainly "create employment"—people would be working fifteen-hour days just to survive. Yet obviously individuals are much better off by having the option to specialize in one occupation, producing far more than they need personally, and trading the surplus with others who are doing the same in their own areas of expertise.

The same principle holds for nations. When different countries specialize in their areas of "comparative advantage" and then trade surplus production with each other, it raises standards of living across the board. It was particularly tragic that the nations of the world decided to sabotage this wonderful cooperation in the midst of the worst economic downturn in modern history.

Making the Depression Great, Step 3: Tax-and-Spend Like a Democrat

Part of the myth of the laissez-faire Hoover holds that he mercilessly slashed the government budget in the early stages of the Depression, because he was wedded to the "classical" free-market doctrines and didn't realize—as modern Keynesians do—that governments are supposed to *boost* spending when the economy goes into a tailspin. This viewpoint was beautifully illustrated in a December 2008 *New York Times* column by Nobel laureate Paul Krugman:

No modern American president would repeat the fiscal mistake of 1932, in which the federal government tried to balance its budget in the face of a severe recession. The Obama administration will put deficit concerns on hold while it fights the economic crisis.

But even as Washington tries to rescue the economy, the nation will be reeling from the actions of 50 Herbert Hoovers—state governors who are slashing spending in a time of recession, often at the expense both of their most vulnerable constituents and of the nation's economic future.

These state-level cutbacks range from small acts of cruelty to giant acts of panic—from cuts in South Carolina's juvenile justice program, which will force young offenders out of group homes and into prison, to the decision by a committee that manages California state spending to halt all construction outlays for six months.

....It's true that the economy is currently shrinking. But that's the result of a slump in private spending. It makes no sense to add to the problem by cutting public spending, too.... The priority right now is to fight off the attack of the 50 Herbert Hoovers, and make sure that the fiscal problems of the states don't make the economic crisis even worse.[18]

Aside from Krugman's characteristic flair for the dramatic, the passages above are impressive because it would be difficult to render a *more* misleading account of Hoover's fiscal policies, without actually lying. First, Hoover did *not* balance the budget—or even come close—in 1932. In Fiscal Year (FY) 1933 (running from July 1, 1932 through June 30, 1933), the federal government ran a deficit of $2.6 billion. To modern ears, that seems quite modest; Henry Paulson handed out more to bankers by breakfast. But Hoover's deficit was the result of spending $4.6 billion while taking in $2 billion in receipts. Thus, as a percentage of revenues, Hoover's profligacy—which remember, Krugman is describing as heartless budget-slashing—was enormous. For comparison, in FY 2007 the federal government would have needed to run a deficit of $3.3 trillion—rather than the actual deficit of $162 billion—to achieve the same proportion of overspending as Hoover did in his allegedly tight-fisted year.

Yet we have only begun to scratch the surface of magician Krugman's misdirection. The only reason the budget deficit was so high—prompting Hoover's tax hikes and budget cuts in FY 1933—was that

Books You're Not Supposed to Read

America's Great Depression, Murray N. Rothbard, Fifth Edition (U.S.A.: The Ludwig von Mises Institute, 2008)

Out of Work: Unemployment and Government in Twentieth-Century America, Richard K. Vedder and Lowell E. Gallaway (New York: New York University Press, 1997)

The Memoirs of Herbert Hoover: The Great Depression, 1929-1941, Herbert Hoover (New York: The Macmillan Company, 1952)

Hoover had behaved as a model Keynesian during his first two years in office. During every single year of the Roaring '20s, the federal government had run budget surpluses, which it used both to justify Mellon's bold tax cuts as well as to retire a large portion of the public debt. (Following the massive borrowing needed for World War I, the federal government paid down its debt from $25.5 billion in FY 1919 to $16.2 billion in FY 1930.)[19] When Hoover came into office, he inherited a sizable surplus of $700 million, which was a hefty sum in relation to a federal budget that was only $3.3 billion. The table below shows what Hoover did with federal finances, after the decade of surpluses (not to mention prosperity) of Calvin Coolidge. (Note that Hoover was sworn in on March 4, 1929, and therefore FY 1930 is more appropriately credited to Calvin Coolidge.)

Federal Receipts, Outlays, and Difference as % of GDP

(historical dollars, billions)

Fiscal Year	Receipts	Outlays	Surplus (+) or Deficit (-)	As % of GDP
July 1929—June 1930	$4.1	$3.3	+$0.7	+0.8%
July 1930—June 1931	$3.1	$3.6	-0.5	-0.6%
July 1931—June 1932	$1.9	$4.7	-2.7	-4.0%
July 1932—June 1933	$2.0	$4.6	-2.6	-4.5%
July 1933—June 1934	$3.0	$6.5	-3.6	-5.9%

Source: The American Presidency Project[20]

Contrary to the impression Krugman gives, the table illustrates that Hoover's response to the stock market crash was an enormous increase in government spending, with the budget exploding by 42 percent over his first two years. This huge surge in spending occurred amidst a collapse in receipts (due both to the decline in economic activity as well as falling prices). Immediately after the crash, Hoover and Mellon also pushed through a temporary one-point reduction in tax rates, applicable to the 1929 tax period.[21] Hoover's handling of the situation was therefore the textbook Keynesian response to a collapse in "aggregate demand."

It is true that eventually Hoover blinked and tried to tame the unprecedented (at the time) peacetime deficits. But this was only after the "stimulus" approach failed horribly. By the time Hoover abandoned the textbook Keynesian remedies in 1932, the unemployment rate had already surpassed 20 percent. Of course, Krugman could contend that this simply proved how bad the situation was, and that Hoover had not been profligate *enough* with his unprecedented spending. Like Hoover himself, Krugman misses the obvious explanation that the unprecedented federal interventions to fight the Depression of the early 1930s were the *cause* of the unprecedented severity of the Depression.

During previous depressions in U.S. history, budget-conscious politicians had slashed spending in reaction to falling tax receipts; they really did behave the way Krugman misleadingly portrayed President Hoover's record. And yet, most Americans cannot associate any of those presidents with their respective depressions, the way everyone knows that "Hoover did nothing to fight the Depression."

As with the evaluation of Hoover's high-wages policy, his high-federal-budget policy can be usefully contrasted with the depression occurring at the end of Woodrow Wilson's watch. With the conclusion of World War I, the U.S. government slashed its budget from $18.5 billion in FY 1919 down to $6.4 billion *one year later*. As the U.S. economy entered a depression at the turn of the decade, receipts fell. The Wilson Administration responded by cutting spending even more, down to $5.0 billion in FY 1921 and then following with a single-year slash of 34 percent, down to $3.3 billion in FY 1922.[22] (Because of the fiscal/calendar year mismatch, it is debatable whether Wilson or Harding should be associated with the FY 1922 budget.)

> ## The Economic Facts of Life
>
> During a depression, when every private citizen is cutting non-essential spending, the government should do so as well.

So how do the two strategies stack up? We already know that Hoover faced 20+ percent unemployment after the second full year of his Keynesian stimulus policies. Wilson/Harding, on the other hand, was Krugman's worst nightmare, taking the axe to federal spending in a way that would have given even Ron Paul the willies, and during a serious depression to boot! Yet as we already know, unemployment peaked at 11.7 percent in 1921, then began falling sharply. The depression was over for Harding, at the corresponding point when a desperate Hoover had decided to (try to) rein in his massive budget deficits.

In fairness, we should concede that there can be no truly controlled experiments in the social sciences. It is theoretically possible that Krugman's interpretation of history is correct. Presumably he would argue that the 1920–21 depression was exacerbated (or perhaps even caused) by the enormous cuts to government spending. And he might further argue that Hoover's profligacy averted unemployment rates of, say, 40 percent in 1931.

But Occam's Razor recommends the simplest answer staring us in the face: the old-school economic wisdom was correct, while the newfangled Keynesian remedies proved disastrous. (For what it's worth, Coolidge never let federal spending exceed $3.3 billion, even though he presided over the most prosperous decade in U.S. history.)[23] During a depression, when every private citizen is cutting nonessential spending, the government should do so as well. The experience of the Harding and Coolidge administrations reminds us that Americans used to treat government as a (huge) business; it could run up debts during emergencies such as war, but then it had to *pay them off* as a matter of fiscal responsibility. This sounds quaint nowadays, brainwashed as the public has been by Keynesian arguments that during periods of belt-tightening, it is the government's duty to spend like a drunken sailor.[24]

Yet we are still not finished undoing the false impression Krugman's essay has given. (His short op-ed is an excellent "make-work" program for those trying to accurately describe the Hoover years.) We now know that Hoover's initial response to the crash was to let federal spending (and the deficit) explode, a strategy that coincided with awful results, in contrast to the classical strategy of belt-tightening which had eliminated almost all earlier U.S. depressions in the same time frame. But even so, couldn't Krugman correctly point out that Hoover's change of heart in

1932 made things worse? After all, the previous table shows that the federal deficit fell slightly from FY 1932 to FY 1933, yet the economy reached the depths of the Depression during this same period. Wasn't it obviously a bad idea for Hoover in 1932 to suddenly get anxious about the federal debt?

To get a full picture of what happened at this lowest of points in U.S. economic history, we need to explore just how Hoover tried to balance the budget. Krugman's quick treatment gives the impression that it was all (heartless) budget cuts. On the contrary, from FY 1932 to FY 1933, the federal budget was cut some $61 million (1.3 percent), while federal receipts increased around $73 million (3.8 percent). Thus, of the slight fall in the (huge) deficit, only 45 percent was due to budget cuts, while the remaining 55 percent was achieved through wringing more out of the taxpayers. Funny, Krugman didn't mention that Hoover raised taxes more than he cut spending when trying to balance the budget.

It gets worse. The figures above convey the impression that Hoover sought a roughly equal mix of tax hikes and budget cuts in order to rein in the red ink. This is completely wrong. It's not as if he bumped up the excise tax on whiskey by 4 percent, and so a few extra points of revenue trickled in. On the contrary, Hoover signed into law *enormous* increases in the *rates* of various taxes. He probably expected tax receipts to go through the roof. But because of the Laffer Curve—where a tax rate increase may yield a much smaller increase in collected revenues, because of the shrinking tax base—the extra yield to the Treasury was modest.

Hoover's tax hikes were astounding. They would have been unconscionable for a president to impose during a period of prosperity; for Hoover to have done so when he did—well, it's no wonder that the period immediately following this decision is the worst in U.S. economic history. As Rothbard describes it:

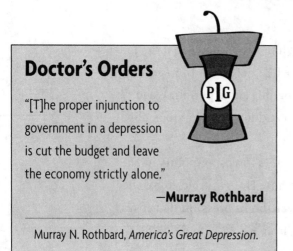

Doctor's Orders

"[T]he proper injunction to government in a depression is cut the budget and leave the economy strictly alone."

—**Murray Rothbard**

Murray N. Rothbard, *America's Great Depression.*

In his swan song as Secretary of Treasury, Andrew Mellon advocated, in December, 1931, drastic increases of taxes, including personal income taxes, estate taxes, sales taxes, and postal rates. Obedient to the lines charted by Mellon and Hoover, Congress passed, in the Revenue Act of 1932, one of the greatest increases in taxation ever enacted in the United States in peacetime. The range of tax increases was enormous. Many wartime excise taxes were revived, sales taxes were imposed on gasoline, tires, autos, electric energy, malt, toiletries, furs, jewelry, and other articles; admission and stock transfer taxes were increased; new taxes were levied on bank checks, bond transfers, telephone, telegraph, and radio messages; and the personal income tax was raised drastically as follows: the normal [brackets were] increased from [an original] range of 1 1/2 percent—5 percent, [up to a new range of] 4 percent—8 percent; personal exemptions were sharply reduced, and an earned credit of 25 percent eliminated; and surtaxes were raised enormously, from a maximum of 25 percent to 63 percent on the highest incomes. Furthermore, the corporate income tax was increased from 12 percent to 13 3/4 percent, and an exemption for small corporations eliminated; the estate tax was doubled, and the exemption floor halved; and the gift tax, which had been eliminated, was restored, and graduated up to 33 1/3 percent.[25]

Federal Tax Schedule 1931

Married Filing Jointly
Marginal Tax Brackets

Tax Rate	Over	But Not Over
1.5%	$0	$4,000
3.0%	$4,000	$8,000
5.0%	$8,000	$10,000
6.0%	$10,000	$14,000
7.0%	$14,000	$16,000
8.0%	$16,000	$18,000
9.0%	$18,000	$20,000
10.0%	$20,000	$22,000
11.0%	$22,000	$24,000
12.0%	$24,000	$28,000
5.1%	$28,000	$32,000
14.0%	$32,000	$36,000
15.0%	$36,000	$40,000
16.0%	$40,000	$44,000
17.0%	$44,000	$48,000
18.0%	$48,000	$52,000
19.0%	$52,000	$56,000
20.0%	$56,000	$60,000
21.0%	$60,000	$64,000
22.0%	$64,000	$70,000
23.0%	$70,000	$80,000
24.0%	$80,000	$100,000
25.0%	$100,000	-

Federal Tax Schedule 1932

Married Filing Jointly
Marginal Tax Brackets

Tax Rate	Over	But Not Over
4.0%	$0	$4,000
8.0%	$4,000	$6,000
9.0%	$6,000	$10,000
10.0%	$10,000	$12,000
11.0%	$12,000	$14,000
12.0%	$14,000	$16,000
13.0%	$16,000	$18,000
14.0%	$18,000	$20,000
16.0%	$20,000	$22,000
17.0%	$22,000	$24,000
18.0%	$24,000	$26,000
19.0%	$26,000	$28,000
20.0%	$28,000	$30,000
21.0%	$30,000	$32,000
23.0%	$32,000	$36,000
24.0%	$36,000	$38,000
25.0%	$38,000	$40,000
26.0%	$40,000	$42,000
27.0%	$42,000	$44,000
28.0%	$44,000	$46,000
29.0%	$46,000	$48,000
30.0%	$48,000	$50,000
31.0%	$50,000	$52,000
32.0%	$52,000	$54,000
33.0%	$54,000	$56,000
34.0%	$56,000	$58,000
35.0%	$58,000	$60,000
36.0%	$60,000	$62,000
37.0%	$62,000	$64,000
38.0%	$64,000	$66,000

Federal Tax Schedule 1931 (continued)
Married Filing Jointly
Marginal Tax Brackets

Federal Tax Schedule 1932 (continued)
Married Filing Jointly
Marginal Tax Brackets

Tax Rate	Over	But Not Over	Tax Rate	Over	But Not Over
			39.0%	$66,000	$68,000
			40.0%	$68,000	$70,000
			41.0%	$70,000	$72,000
			42.0%	$72,000	$74,000
			43.0%	$74,000	$76,000
			44.0%	$76,000	$78,000
			45.0%	$78,000	$80,000
			46.0%	$80,000	$82,000
			47.0%	$82,000	$84,000
			48.0%	$84,000	$86,000
			49.0%	$86,000	$88,000
			50.0%	$88,000	$90,000
			51.0%	$90,000	$92,000
			52.0%	$92,000	$94,000
			53.0%	$94,000	$96,000
			54.0%	$96,000	$98,000
			55.0%	$98,000	$100,000
			56.0%	$100,000	$150,000
			57.0%	$150,000	$200,000
			58.0%	$200,000	$300,000
			59.0%	$300,000	$400,000
			60.0%	$400,000	$500,000
			61.0%	$500,000	$750,000
			62.0%	$750,000	$1,000,000
			63.0%	$1,000,000	

Source: Tax Foundation[26]

Paul Krugman is right to warn politicians not to repeat the fiscal mistakes of Herbert Hoover. Hoover showed that huge increases in federal spending wouldn't rescue an economy from depression, and that massive tax hikes only added insult to injury. At the risk of boring the reader, we point out once again that Treasury Secretary Mellon pursued the opposite program in the 1920s, and the result was prosperity.

Making the Depression Great, Step 4: Install a New Deal-Lite

We have seen that Herbert Hoover departed drastically from the laissez-faire policies attributed to him by most modern Americans. Yet the irony runs deeper, for Hoover's strategy for fighting the Depression looks very similar, if in scaled-down form, to FDR's New Deal that allegedly "got us out of the Depression." With some notable exceptions (such as their positions vis-à-vis the gold standard), FDR's plan for recovery could be described as Herbert Hoover Squared. A brief discussion of Hoover's farm supports, public works expenditures, and Reconstruction Finance Corporation—which were only part of Hoover's New Deal Lite—will suffice to make the point.

Murray Rothbard argues that if one looks at content, rather than labels, then a fair case can be made that the "New Deal" program of farm intervention began under Herbert Hoover, not Franklin Roosevelt. Hoover had supported the farm bloc throughout his political career, and during his first presidential campaign promised he would institute a price-support

---

FDR Was Right—But Then What Did He Do?

In the 1932 presidential race, Franklin Roosevelt railed against his opponent's spending, calling the Hoover Administration "the most reckless and extravagant past that I have been able to discover in the statistical record of any peacetime government anywhere, any time."

Quoted in Burton Folsom, Jr., *New Deal or Raw Deal?*, 40.

program. He proved true to his word in June 1929 (three months after he was sworn in as president) with the creation of the Federal Farm Board (FFB). The FFB was initially allocated $500 million to give low-interest rate loans to farm cooperatives, and it also had the power (through corporations that it created) to buy surplus farm products off the market and hence prop up their prices. (Hoover won an additional $100 million for the FFB in the spring of 1930.)[27]

Good Advice

Issuing more government debt for huge public works programs "would encroach seriously, and perhaps dangerously upon the supply of capital funds that private enterprise will need in order to help the country climb out of depression again."

—Metropolitan Life Insurance Company economist **William A. Berridge**, 1932

Quoted in Murray N. Rothbard, *America's Great Depression*, 293.

As usual, throwing tax dollars at the problem only made it worse. In a market economy, if a particular group of producers, even the cherished farmer, can't make a living, then it means there are too many people in that line of work. Heartless as it sounds, the only sustainable solution to the problem of inadequate farm income was for the least efficient farmers to find other careers. Actual and promised government "support" allowed these marginal producers to limp along, so that there really *was* overproduction in the subsidized crops. (This is different from the belief of Hoover and others that the Depression was due to a *general* overproduction. The FFB actually channeled too many resources into farming, leading to overproduction in that sector but *under*production elsewhere.) Realizing that its practice of "buy high, sell low" was wasting tax dollars, and that the price supports were leading to ever-growing stockpiles in government silos, the FFB took the next "logical" step of ordering output restrictions (while maintaining price supports!). Rothbard describes the results of this attempt to overturn economic law:

[C]onfronted with growing surpluses, and therefore heavier pressure on farm prices...the FFB tried to exhort the cotton farmers...to reduce acreage. Chairman Stone, of the FFB, urged the governors of the cotton states to "immediately mobilize every interested and available agency...to induce immediate plowing under of every third row of cotton now growing." This action stirred up a host of indignant opposition, the *New York Times* calling it "one of the maddest things that ever came from an official body." The proposal met with no success; in fact the 1931 cotton crop was considerably larger. In early 1932, the Board then tried an heroic action— along with its 1.3 million bales, it obtained an agreement from southern bankers to withhold all of their cotton (3.5 million bales), while it continued to finance 2.1 million bales held by the coops. This firmed prices until June 1932, when they fell drastically again.

Bad Advice

"Just as we saved our way into depression, we must squander our way out of it."

—*Business Week* economist **Virgil Jordan**, 1932

Quoted in Murray N. Rothbard, *America's Great Depression*, 291.

By July, the Board had bought $127 million worth of cotton, and it had lost over half of its value. The upshot was that the [Cotton Stabilization Corporation] had to give up, and it began to liquidate its cotton holdings in August, 1932, completing its unloading in a year. The net loss of cotton was $16 million, in addition to 850,000 bales, worth over $78 million, donated to the Red Cross.[28]

Generous subsidies and output restrictions in agriculture were not the only components of Hoover's New Deal Lite. At this point, it should not surprise the reader to learn that within weeks of the stock market crash,

Hoover spearheaded a massive increase in public works spending. On November 23, 1929, he sent a telegram to all of the governors, and won their cooperation in expanding state-level spending. On the federal level, Hoover asked Congress to boost the budget of the Federal Buildings program more than $400 million, and also requested an additional $175 million (for public works projects) for the Shipping Board. Hoover did all of this before year's end, prompting Columbia economics professor J. M. Clark to praise the president's "great experiment in constructive industrial statesmanship of a promising and novel sort."[29] In July 1930, Congress authorized an enormous $915 million public works program,[30] which as a percentage of the economy translates to $149 billion in 2007. Rothbard notes that the older Hoover "still points out proudly that the aggregate public works of the four years of his administration was greater than the public works in the entire previous 30 years," and that Hoover "still takes credit for launching, in this period, Jones Beach, the San Francisco Bay Bridge, the Los Angeles Aqueduct, and Boulder [Hoover] Dam."[31]

Sounds like Obama

"[W]e might have done nothing. That would have been utter ruin. Instead, we met the situation with proposals to private business and to Congress of the most gigantic program of economic defense and counterattack ever evolved in the history of the Republic. We put it into action."

—**Herbert Hoover**'s acceptance speech for the Republican 1932 presidential nomination

Quoted in Murray N. Rothbard, *America's Great Depression*, 321.

We come to our last exhibit in the case for Hoover's New Deal Lite: the Reconstruction Finance Corporation. Suppose 100 American college seniors were asked, "During the 1930s, which American president established the Reconstruction Finance Corporation, which lent $1 billion in its first five months of operation to prop up unhealthy banks and railroads?" Probably not one would answer, "Herbert Hoover."

Created in early 1932, the RFC was an important plank in Hoover's recovery plan. In that year it extended credits of $2.3 billion, and advanced more than $1.5 billion in cash.[32] The program, flawed in itself, was made worse by the almost inevitable corruption attending Hoover's pet program. Historian Burt Folsom writes:

> When Hoover used $1.5 billion of taxpayer money to pick winners and losers of special government loans, the process was quickly and inevitably politicized. Those with the right political connections found themselves at the head of the line. For example, the treasurer of the Republican National Committee received a loan of $14 million for his bank in Cleveland. In one of the worst cases, Charles Dawes, the head of the RFC (and a former Republican vice president) resigned from the RFC just in time to win a $90 million loan for his Chicago bank. Hoover's administration, therefore, was so mired in questionable economic decisions that it had no credible offensive against Roosevelt [in the 1932 campaign].[33]

Herbert Hoover: A Big Government Man

The idea that Herbert Hoover was a staunch small-government man is a complete myth. (The one area where he was a small government man is one not often mentioned by his liberal critics: he wanted defense spending and military interventions kept to a minimum.) Hoover consciously, proudly, broke ranks with laissez-faire economists and with every president before him, implementing the largest peacetime expansion of government in U.S. history (at least to that point). In the midst of a depression, he propped up wage rates to help the working man, only to produce the largest glut on the labor market in its history—something that any competent economist could have predicted. So where did the myth of the laissez-faire Hoover come from? Was it fabricated out of whole cloth?

Not really. For one thing, in the 1932 presidential campaign, Herbert Hoover really was the more "conservative" of the candidates—though this proves little since his opponent was a fascist (and I am using that loaded and overused term in its strict economic definition)—and Hoover feared for the nation if it followed the course that the charismatic FDR was charting. [34] It is also true that during his administration, Hoover resisted calls for direct relief to the unemployed from the federal government; Hoover preferred that local governments and voluntary charities help the

Who Needs Keynes When You Have Hoover?

"I determined that it was my duty, even without precedent, to call upon the business of the country for coordinated and constructive action to resist the forces of disintegration. The business community, the bankers, labor, and the government have cooperated in wider spread measures of mitigation than have ever been attempted before.... Our leading business concerns have sustained wages, have distributed employment, have expedited heavy construction. The Government has expanded public works, assisted in credit to agriculture, and has restricted immigration. These measures have maintained a higher degree of consumption than would otherwise have been the case. They have thus prevented a large measure of unemployment.... Our present experience in relief should form the basis of even more amplified plans in the future."

—**Herbert Hoover**, address to American Bankers' Association, October 1930.

Quoted in Murray N. Rothbard, *America's Great Depression*, 244–45.

indigent. Reading his memoirs, one gets the sense that Hoover—unlike the Court-packing FDR—took seriously the limits of the U.S. Constitution, even if he felt the federalist system handcuffed his efforts to "do something" (such as curbing the stock market bubble when he first took office[35]). Finally, modern-day critics of Hoover are certainly correct to accuse him of subordinating other policy aims to maintenance of the gold standard—though this desire to uphold Uncle Sam's obligations to creditors and all holders of dollars is surely a *virtue* on Hoover's part.

In truth, Herbert Hoover was not the dogmatic right-winger taught in many history classes, but neither was he a central planner. Indeed, Herbert Hoover's views on the proper role of the federal government are remarkably "modern," in contrast to some of the truly extreme elements of the Roosevelt Administrations who looked with approval on the model of Soviet Russia, something Hoover certainly did not. Hoover's nuanced worldview is summed up well in the following excerpt from his correspondence of February 1933:

> We can say, without qualification, that the motivation of production based on private initiative has proved the very mother of plenty. It has faults, for humanity is not without faults. Difficulties arise from overexpansion and adjustment to the march of labor-saving devices, but in broad result it stands in sharp contrast with the failure of the system of production, as in its greater exemplar—Russia—where after fifteen years of trial, in a land of as great natural resources as ours, that system has never produced in a single year an adequate supply of even the barest necessities in food and clothing for its people....
>
> [Our] system moves supplies of everything into remotest villages and crossroads; it feeds and clothes great cities each day with the regularity and assurance which cause never a thought or anxiety. The diffusion of commodities and services

in a social sense has faults. In normal times out of our 120,000,000 people there are a few millions who conscientiously work and strive, yet do not receive that minimum of commodities and services to which they have a just right as earnest members of the community.

There is another fringe of a few hundred thousand who receive more than they deserve for the effort they make. But taxes are furnishing rapid correction in this quarter....The enlarging social sense of our people is furnishing the impulse to correction of faults....It is not to be brought about by destruction of the system.[36]

Chapter 3

DID THE TIGHTWAD FED'S DEFLATION CAUSE THE GREAT DEPRESSION?

In addition to the myth of the laissez-faire Herbert Hoover, another popular theory of the Great Depression blames the do-nothing Federal Reserve. Ironically, this interpretation comes, not from Big Government critics of the free market, but instead from none other than Milton Friedman and his monetarist followers. Just as modern-day Keynesians urge the government to "avoid the mistakes of Hoover" by running up massive deficits, so too do modern monetarists urge the Fed to "avoid the mistakes of the Depression" by injecting massive amounts of reserves into the banking system.

The parallels between the myth of the laissez-faire Hoover and the myth of the do-nothing Fed are striking. Just as Hoover engaged in unprecedented "stimulus" through his fiscal policies, so too did the Fed—starting immediately after the stock market crash in 1929—engage in unprecedented "easy money" policies. Because the massive budget deficits eventually forced Hoover to reverse course and raise taxes (in 1932), modern Keynesians say Hoover didn't borrow-and-spend *enough*. Similarly, because a gold outflow from the country eventually forced the Fed to reverse course and tighten the money supply (in late 1931), the monetarists say the Fed didn't inflate *enough*. But in both cases, the question remains: If budget deficits and cheap money were the right medicine,

Guess What?

- Falling prices can be a sign of prosperity

- There was sharper deflation in earlier depressions than in the 1930s

- The Fed tried an "easy money" approach after the stock market crash

why was the Depression still getting worse, two years into these unprecedented fiscal and monetary remedies?

The reader surely knows that the myth of the do-nothing Hoover animates today's calls for Congress to spend more. But the reader may not be aware that the myth of the do-nothing Fed *also* motivates policymakers today. In fact, before assuming his current role as chairman of the Federal Reserve, then-Fed governor Ben Bernanke said in his 2002 birthday tribute to Milton Friedman: "Let me end my talk by abusing slightly my status as an official representative of the Federal Reserve. I would like to say to Milton and Anna: Regarding the Great Depression. You're right, we did it. We're very sorry. But thanks to you, we won't do it again."[1]

The myth of the do-nothing Fed is what has guided Ben Bernanke's response to the modern financial crisis. During the last three months of 2008, the Fed expanded bank reserves at an annualized rate of more than *400,000* percent.[2] (This—or anything remotely like it—has never happened before in the history of the Fed.) If Friedman's hypothesis is correct, then Bernanke's astronomical injections of liquidity are the right course of action. But if it turns out that Friedman was *wrong* to blame the Depression on deflation and the do-nothing Fed, then the United States economy may be on the verge of breaking some more records (and not good ones).

Friedman: The Timid Fed and Deflation in the 1930s

Milton Friedman and Anna Schwartz laid out their theory in their classic 1963 work, *A Monetary History of the United States*. Their argument was that the powerful Governor of the New York Federal Reserve Bank, Benjamin Strong, had been very competent as the de facto head of the entire Federal Reserve until his death in 1928. But after his departure, bureaucratic infighting and sheer incompetence led to disaster. Friedman gives a layman's summary in his (also classic) *Free to Choose*:

[The] depressing effects of the stock market crash were strongly reinforced by the subsequent behavior of the Federal Reserve System. At the time of the crash, the New York Federal Reserve Bank, almost by conditioned reflex instilled during the Strong era, immediately acted on its own to cushion the shock by purchasing government securities, thereby adding to bank reserves. That enabled commercial banks to cushion the shock by providing additional loans to stock market firms and purchasing securities from them and others affected adversely by the crash. But Strong *was* dead, and the Board wanted to establish its leadership. It moved rapidly to impose its discipline on [the] New York [Federal Reserve Bank], and New York yielded. Thereafter the System acted very differently than it had during earlier economic recessions in the 1920s. Instead of actively expanding the money supply by more than the usual amount to offset the contraction, the System allowed the quantity of money to decline slowly throughout 1930. Compared to the decline of roughly one-third in the quantity of money from late 1930 to early 1933, the decline in the quantity of money up to October 1930 seems mild—a mere 2.6 percent. However, compared with past episodes, it was sizable. Indeed, it was a larger decline than had occurred during or preceding all but a few of the earlier recessions.[3]

To illustrate that this is not merely a technical debate that has been confined to professional economists, we note that historian and Cato Institute scholar Jim Powell endorsed the Friedman theory in his (excellent) popular book on the New Deal. After quoting Friedman and Schwartz's description of the Fed's rate hike in August 1929 to curb the speculative boom, Powell writes:

The October 1929 stock crash made clear that the Fed had overplayed its hand. . . . Without realizing that one measure is having an effect not yet apparent, an anxious central banker could authorize another action that ended up compounding a problem and disrupting the entire economy.

These Federal Reserve policies began a monetary contraction. As the contraction became more severe, it brought on a depression in output, employment, and income. If nothing else had happened, there would have been a depression because of the severe monetary contraction.[4]

The problem with this explanation is that the Fed did try to inflate after the crash to rescue the economy, adopting unprecedented measures of "easy money" in 1930–1931, precisely when Powell (following Friedman) accuses the Fed of allowing a monetary contraction that yielded a depression. Moreover, the falling prices that correspond to a tighter money supply are not necessarily harmful to the economy.

The monetarists are right in laying much of the blame for the Great Depression on the Federal Reserve—but for the wrong reasons. The Fed's fault was *not* in providing too little liquidity; rather, its fault was flooding the credit markets in the 1920s, and then, after the stock market crash, in propping up unsound enterprises with even cheaper money. Economies recover from recessions or depressions by reallocating labor and capital to their most efficient uses. Propping up ailing industries only delays that necessary process and thereby deepens the weaknesses of an economy and delays recovery. The printing press does not create wealth; it creates green pieces of paper featuring U.S. presidents. The contraction of the early 1930s was the economy's attempt to recuperate from the earlier *bubble* inflated by the Fed—the proper role for the authorities at this late stage was to stay out of it, not to embark on another spree of dollar-printing.

Who's Afraid of Falling Prices?

We've all—wrongly—been trained to fear falling prices, now known as *deflation*. (Just as with the term *inflation*, the definition has morphed over time; originally *deflation* referred to a shrinking money supply, which of course tended to reduce prices.) In fact, many Americans have come to identify the very term *depression* to include "falling prices," rather than simply, "a very severe recession in economic activity," because one thing we remember about the Great Depression is that prices fell. It's not surprising, then, that Americans believe the talking heads on CNBC when they warn of the evils of deflation, and recommend that the Federal Reserve flood the markets with new money just to be on the safe side. Peter Bernstein recalls the great deflation scare of the early 2000s:

> This [dot-com] recession, mild as it may have been, brought the economy perilously close to slipping into deflation. In early 2002, the CPI [Consumer Price Index] was crawling along at annual rates close to 1%, compared with more than 3% a year earlier. Greenspan and the Open Market Committee agreed that deflation would be the worst possible outcome, as Japan's disastrous experience in the 1980s had demonstrated so dramatically. Once consumers and business managers begin to anticipate lower prices, they postpone their purchases as long as they can—a decision that only makes the price declines even steeper and more difficult to reverse.[5]

We focus here on Bernstein's remarks not to single him out for criticism, but because he has so succinctly captured the dominant view of deflation, which is quite simply nonsensical.

For starters, notice that Bernstein's actual argument is that the problem with deflation is that it leads to...more deflation. But unless we first know *why* deflation is bad, that is hardly a strike against it. Heroin use leads to more heroin use, and that is presumably a bad path to follow, but listening to classical music tends to reinforce the habit, and that is presumably a noble practice. If the reader finds our point to be flippant, consider this: Bernstein (echoing Greenspan) wants inflation. But after twisting a few knobs on Bernstein's warning, we can say with just as much validity: "Once consumers and business managers begin to anticipate *higher* prices, they *accelerate* their purchases as *quickly* as they can—a decision that only makes the price *hikes* even steeper and more difficult to reverse." If Bernstein has demonstrated the black hole of deflation, we have just demonstrated the supernova of inflation.

Bernstein could give the obvious response that deflation is worse than inflation because it's better to have people spending than hoarding. After all, businesses can't sell their products or keep people employed if everybody is holding out for bigger price cuts. But this (typical) argument proves too much. One could construct an analogous argument for the computer industry, in which the government passes regulation to slow down improvements in operating systems and processor speed. After all, how can computer manufacturers possibly remain viable if consumers are always waiting for a faster model to become available? What consumer would be foolish enough to spend money on a laptop when it will be obsolete in six months? The solution to this paradox, of course, is that consumers *do* decide to bite the bullet and buy a computer, knowing full well that they would be able to buy the same performance for less money, if they were willing to wait. This truism doesn't paralyze computer buyers, because if consistently followed the rule would never allow a person to buy a computer at all. The "deflation" that has always characterized the personal computer industry—that is, ever stronger computers getting ever cheaper to buy—is a sign of its health, not an explanation for its sickness.

But for the sake of argument, let us grant that falling prices cause many consumers to delay buying big-ticket items. This still does not prove that

business sales in general will suffer. Suppose a man had planned on buying a new car for $20,000, but the local car dealership has bought far too
much inventory and the man expects his desired car will sell for $19,000
in three months. It is certainly worth it for the man to wait 90 days and
earn, in essence, $1,000 for his patience. But it is even more lucrative for
him to wait 90 days and earn $1,250, by reaping the $1,000 from the
falling car price, but also using the three-month window to earn $250 in
interest by putting his $20,000 into bank CDs yielding a 5 percent annual
return.

As this example illustrates, falling prices don't encourage hoarding per
se, they rather encourage *saving*. Many analysts who are terrified of deflation stress that in an environment of falling prices, cash stuffed under the
mattress earns a positive return. This observation is certainly true, but
nonetheless cash lent out earns an even greater return. Falling prices,
then, encourage consumers to devote more of their income to savings,
which in turn lowers interest rates and allows businesses to borrow and
invest more. In effect, by postponing their big-ticket purchases, consumers free up resources so that businesses can buy more of *their* big-
ticket items (a new copier, a new warehouse, and so on). One might
wonder why businesses would borrow and invest if consumers are not
spending on products, but we point again to the personal computer
industry: if the price declines are expected to last, then at some point
consumers will begin buying again. (There's no point in holding out for
lower prices but never actually buying!) On the other hand, if the price
declines are considered temporary, then consumers will begin buying
again once they hit bottom. In either case, the mere fact of deflation
doesn't paralyze business investment; consumers are buying fewer products today so that they can buy more products down the road.

There is one final argument for the alleged evils of deflation that we
can quickly dispatch. The claim runs like this: in a deflationary environment, production comes to a standstill because profits get squeezed out

of existence. After all, businesses make profits by buying the materials they need to produce their products and then selling the finished goods at a markup. But with falling prices, the producer's margin gets eliminated, turning a profit to a loss. So rather than tying up capital in a process that loses money, businesses will choose to earn a positive "real" return by sitting on their cash.

The problem here is that the argument mixes apples and oranges. Even if the prices of both raw materials and finished goods are constantly falling, producers can still make a profit so long as their materials are cheaper today than what the *finished goods* will fetch at the time of sale. Suppose over the course of five years, prices fall by half. In the year 2009, a bottle of wine (aged 5 years) sells for $40, while the total price for grapes and everything else needed to make a bottle of the wine is $10. Even though all prices will be cut in half by 2014, it still pays to spend $10 in 2009 buying the grapes in order to have a 5-year-old bottle of wine ready to sell for $20 in 2014. It's true that the price of the raw materials will have fallen to $5 by 2014, but that's irrelevant—you buy the grapes in order to make *wine*, not to sell the grapes after sitting on them for five years. The wine producer's original $10 investment still yields him a profit of $10 a bottle, even though we chose the numbers to reflect consistent and large deflation. By itself, in an otherwise healthy economy, deflation should be no more disruptive than inflation.

Deflation: Historical Evidence

During the heyday of the classical gold standard in the nineteenth century, industrialized countries often experienced periods of prosperity that went hand-in-hand with falling prices. In fact, there was consistent deflation in the United States for several years *before* the stock market crash. In 1926, consumer prices fell 2.2 percent, in 1927 they fell another 1.1 percent, and in 1928 they fell yet another 1.2 percent.[6] Falling prices spread the wealth in a more efficient way than Barack Obama's heavy hand of government possibly can. For example, Henry Ford's Model T sold for $600 in 1912 but its price had fallen to $240 by the mid-1920s,[7] putting car ownership within the reach of many more Americans, whose take-home incomes were growing rapidly thanks to increased productivity and lower tax rates. To hear some modern analysts discuss deflation, one would think the 1926 to 1928 period should have been awful for business. Yet this obviously wasn't the case.

Even the deflation following the 1929 crash wasn't the worst on record. From November 1929 to November 1930, prices fell 5.2 percent. Then from November 1930 to November 1931, they fell an additional 10.4 percent, and then a further 10.2 percent through November 1932. (Prices finally hit bottom in March 1933 and soon after began rising.) These are sobering figures, to be sure. But let us once again contrast the Great Depression experience with the earlier 1920–1921 depression. From their peak in June 1920, prices fell 15.8 percent over the next twelve months, a one-year deflation that was 50 percent more severe than any 12-month fall during the Great Depression. And yet, the 1920–1921 depression was so short-lived that most Americans today are unaware of its existence.

Those terrified of deflation might play one last card: "True, the one-year fall in 1920–1921 was steeper than anything in the 1930s, but it was over before people's expectations really changed. The severe and persistent deflation in the early 1930s was what really sealed the doom of the American economy."

Well, actually, no. History tells us otherwise. Between 1839 and 1843 the money supply fell by 34 percent and wholesale prices fell by 42 percent.[8] If the monetarists are right, and it was the Fed's refusal to counteract the falling money supply in the early 1930s that gave us the Great Depression, then the 1839–1843 period should have been devastating. Yet Murray Rothbard (relying on Peter Temin's historical research) reports otherwise:

Books You're Not Supposed to Read

The Ethics of Money Production, Jörg Guido Hülsmann (Auburn, AL: The Ludwig von Mises Institute, 2008)

A Monetary History of the United States, Milton Friedman and Anna Schwartz (Princeton, N.J.: Princeton University Press, 1963)

Less Than Zero: The Case for a Falling Price Level in a Growing Economy, George Selgin (London: Institute of Economic Affairs, 1997)

[T]he effects on real production of the two deflations were very different. Whereas in 1929–1933, real gross investment fell catastrophically by 91 percent, real consumption by 19 percent, and real GNP by 30 percent; in 1839–1843, investment fell by 23 percent, but real consumption *increased* by 21 percent and real GNP by 16 percent.[9]

One shouldn't make too much of such comparisons, because the integrity of macroeconomic data becomes more suspect the farther back we look. Even so, it is safe to say that the deflation (whether defined as a fall in the money supply or a fall in prices) of the early 1930s, though severe, was not unprecedented in American history—and yet the economy suffered far more in the 1930s. The logical conclusion is that deflation and tight money supply were not the problem—or at least not the primary problem—during the Great Depression. To understand the causes of this most awful period in U.S. economic history, we need to look elsewhere.

But Why Would the Fed Destroy Money?

Casual readers who stumble across the monetarist explanation may draw the false conclusion that the Fed consciously sucked one-third of the dollars out of the economy after the stock market crash, in which case it seems a no-brainer that "the Fed's deflation caused the Depression." However, that is not what happened. Rather, the Fed tried unprecedented measures to bolster the financial sector, but its efforts were overwhelmed by the public's behavior, which, naturally, was to hoard money. The resulting decline in the money stock was therefore a tidal wave that the Fed could not contain, as opposed to a conscious policy decision by the Fed. The Federal Reserve authorities actually don't have the power to determine the total amount of money in the economy, because of the fractional reserve banking system.

Under this system, the banks are legally required to keep only a small percentage (say, 10 percent) of their customers' cash deposits as a reserve to "back" total checking deposits. Ignoring some complications, this means that if the banks have $50 billion collectively in their vaults as cash, then the total money supply in the economy is actually closer to $500 billion, because most merchants accept checks (or debit card transactions) drawn on commercial banks just as easily as they accept currency. In a fractional reserve banking system, the $50 billion in actual, printed currency can do the work of $500 billion in pushing up prices in the economy.

This inflationary multiplier is reversed during a panic, when depositors withdraw their funds from checking accounts in order to have more liquid currency on hand. For example, if a depositor becomes spooked—perhaps he fears a bank run—and withdraws his entire checking balance of $1,000 to hold as physical currency, then his action will ultimately *destroy* $9,000 worth of money in the economy. Because the man reduced his bank's cash reserves (in the vault) by $1,000, the bank must reduce its total outstanding checking deposits by $10,000. It can accomplish this through nonrenewal of short-term loans, and by leaning on borrowers to repay their funds to the bank. But in any case, the man's decision to withdraw has reduced the total money supply in the community by $9,000, which will lead to a fall in prices (other things constant).

This is why monetarists assert that the Fed didn't do enough in the early 1930s to counteract the deflationary side-effect from scared depositors withdrawing funds. Yet it is ironic to accuse the Fed of doing too little to fight deflation, when it flooded the system with very cheap money, to an extent it had never done before in previous economic downturns.

Propping up Losers

To modern readers, it seems natural that during a financial panic, the Fed would adopt a loose policy. However, at the time of the stock market crash this effort to "provide a soft landing" to troubled firms was a new and improved medicine for an ailing financial sector—just as President Hoover was busy implementing his own revolutionary remedies. As opposed to the Fed's innovative easy-money approach to depression in the 1930s, the traditional remedy was summed up by Walter Bagehot's famous dictum for the Bank of England in the late 19th century: In a crisis, discount freely *but at a high rate of discount*.[10] In other words: the central bank should be prepared to loan as much as businesses wish to borrow, but only if they can put up good collateral and only if they are willing to pay a steep price.

This classical tough-love policy forced businessmen to be honest with themselves. If a firm were fundamentally sound but temporarily illiquid, it would be eligible for central bank loans and would be willing to pay the high interest rate on them. On the other hand, the people running firms that had no long-term future would realize the jig was up, and they would declare bankruptcy. This would cause temporary pain, to be sure, especially for the workers employed at these unprofitable businesses. But when the economy falls into a recession, it means that too many resources and workers are employed in the *wrong* places. Unpleasant as it is, the best way to deal with the problem is a quick and severe burst of business failures, to release assets and labor to other, profitable firms.

This traditional central bank medicine worked fairly well, inasmuch as American history students don't study any catastrophic worldwide depressions occurring in the nineteenth century. By now the reader will not be surprised to learn that during the *Great* Depression, the Fed and other central banks decided to try a kinder, gentler approach rather than the stern liquidationist strategy of the past. Writing in 1934, economist Lionel Robbins noted:

> In the present depression we have changed all that. We eschew the sharp purge. We prefer the lingering disease. Everywhere, in the money market, in the commodity markets and in the broad field of company finance and public indebtedness, the efforts of Central Banks and Governments have been directed to propping up bad business positions.
>
> We can see this most vividly in the sphere of Central Banking policy. The moment the boom broke in 1929, the Central Banks of the world, acting obviously in concert, set to work to create a condition of easy money, quite out of relation to the general conditions of the money market. This policy was backed up by vigorous purchases of securities in the open market in the United States of America. From October 1929 to December 1930 no less than $410 million was pumped in the market in this way. The result was as might have been expected. The process of liquidation was arrested. New loans were floated.[11]

Robbins' description may surprise readers who are familiar with the monetarist explanation of the Great Depression. Nonetheless, the facts show that the Fed adopted an easy-money policy after the stock market crash. Various authors use different proxies for assessing Fed policy, and at this early period the very term "Fed policy" is a bit of a misnomer because the individual Reserve Banks enjoyed far more autonomy than they do today. In the interest of picking a straightforward and consistent measure, for our purposes we will rely on the discount rate charged by the

Federal Reserve Bank of New York.[12] (The discount rate is the interest rate that the Fed charges on loans it makes directly to banks, which put up some of their assets as collateral.) When it opened for business in November 1914, the (New York) Fed set its discount rate at 6 percent. From that starting point, the Fed's discount rate varied, but never strayed below 3 percent.

In 1927, Great Britain was experiencing an alarming drain on its gold reserves, because it had pegged the British pound to gold at the pre-war parity, even though it had printed too much money during the war for this to be feasible. In order to take the pressure off the pound, the Fed lowered rates in 1927, which had the effect of increasing the supply of dollars and halted the outflow of gold from Britain. But this move fueled the stock market bubble, and the alarmed New York Fed began raising rates again in February 1928, reaching 6 percent by October 1929.

On November 1, 1929, just three days after Wall Street's Black Tuesday, the Fed slashed its discount rate by a full percentage point. Then fifteen days later it cut again, to 4 1/2 percent. Throughout the following year, it cut five more times, so that by December 1930 the New York Fed's discount rate had fallen to 2 percent. This was already a record-low for the Fed, but it cut further still, reaching 1 1/2 percent in May 1931. The Fed only reversed course and began hiking rates in October 1931, after Great Britain (the month before) abandoned the gold standard and Federal Reserve authorities needed to staunch an outflow of gold from the country by panicked world investors.

So we see that immediately following the stock market crash, the Fed began flooding the market with liquidity and in fact brought its rates down *to record lows*. Of course, those who blame the Fed for providing insufficient liquidity may say of these cuts, "too little, too late." But there's a problem with this: If the ostensible *cause* of the Great Depression—the one factor that set it apart from all previous depressions—was the Fed's unwillingness to provide sufficient liquidity, then how could it possibly be that the Fed's *record* rate cuts proved inadequate to solve "the problem?"

This is a crucial point, so let us restate it: Those who argue that the Fed's stinginess turned a typical depression into the Great Depression would have a plausible case if (say) the Fed cut rates after the crash in 1929, but only modestly, and not nearly to the same degree as it had cut rates during previous crises. If those were the facts, *then* it might make sense to argue that the Fed's lack of aggressiveness allowed the depression to fester into the Great one. But those *aren't* the facts; the Fed cuts after the stock market crash in 1929 through September 1931 were not modest, they were at the time the most aggressive in its history.

Now perhaps there is more to the story than simple rate cuts. For example, some economists, following the monetarist explanation, have blamed the Fed for crowding out private efforts to rescue the banking system. In other words, before the Fed opened its doors in 1914, it was customary in a financial panic for private financiers and clearinghouses to coordinate and give assistance to solvent but illiquid banks, which were under pressure from customer withdrawals. Yet these private-sector solutions were hindered after the creation of the mighty Federal Reserve, as these liquid private groups held back and "waited forlornly for the rescue that never came."[13]

Although it is undeniable that the creation of the Fed paralyzed private-sector "lender of last resort" efforts, this factor by itself doesn't really explain the Great Depression. To see why, we draw from our old workhorse, the 1920–1921 depression—a severe contraction that occurred when the Fed had been "on the job" for six years. If the unprecedented rate cuts in the early 1930s were insufficient help to the banks because the Fed had scared away private-sector relief efforts, then the Fed's harsh rate *hike* in 1920–1921—which we are about to describe—should have proved catastrophic, since the Fed's presence should have also crippled private-sector rescues during this period.

The expansion of the money supply during World War I had led to unconscionable consumer price inflation, which was running at more than 20 percent by late 1919. Consequently, the (New York) Fed hiked its discount rate from 4.75 percent up to 6 percent in one fell swoop in January 1920. The Fed then hiked again to a record-high 7 percent in June 1920. Despite the fairly severe depression—recall that unemployment

How Could Milton Friedman Have Been So Wrong?

Milton Friedman was a gifted economist, and often right, but his famous monetarist explanation of the Great Depression is dead wrong. In previous depressions, the United States had experienced severer deflation and collapses in the money supply *without* suffering the economic devastation of the Great Depression. More problematic still for Friedman's theory, the Fed hiked rates to record highs during the 1920–1921 depression, while the Fed cut rates to record lows during the early 1930s. So how could Friedman end up attributing the intensity of the Great Depression to a tightwad Fed?

The most immediate answer is that Friedman (and co-author Anna Schwartz) built their case on other evidence, and did not directly confront the challenges posed above. For example, Friedman could correctly point to incipient recessions during the 1920s that were nipped in the bud with Fed rate cuts. The stock market crashed after the Fed repeatedly *hiked* rates in 1928 and 1929, and so Friedman naturally concluded that low rates successfully kept depression at bay, whereas the foolish rate hikes invited disaster.

Another major argument for the Friedman camp was the apparent connection between recovery from the Great Depression and the abandonment of the gold standard. Other countries severed their currencies' ties to gold earlier than the United States, and they pulled out of the Depression more quickly. Focusing just on the American experience, the major economic

averaged 11.7 percent in 1921—the Fed held steady to its record-high rate for almost a full year, not cutting until May 1921, after the depression was basically over.

Thus, surveying the entire period from its founding in 1914 through 1931, the New York Federal Reserve Bank's record-high discount rate occurred only during the 1920–1921 depression, and its record-low

indicators all turned around—at least temporarily—almost the moment Roosevelt took office and broke the dollar's tie to gold.

Although Friedman's arguments are superficially plausible, they miss the "big picture," which is that the Fed's rate cuts in the mid-1920s weren't wise policy, but rather kept the price of capital too low—lower than free market rates would have been—and thus fueled a boom that had to go bust at some point. By the same token, the Fed's rate hikes late in the decade didn't push down the stock market, but instead stopped inflating it. When the Fed stopped pumping in so much cheap credit, the stock market naturally fell back to a more natural level.

The rapid infusion of new money following the abandonment of the gold standard may have given a temporary appearance of prosperity, but it certainly did not solve the world's economic troubles, which lingered through the Second World War. After the worldwide credit bubble had popped in 1929, the major economies *should* have experienced a severe depression while resources were shuffled into more appropriate and sustainable lines. The gold standard kept central banks honest, and allowed falling prices to signal the bleak news to everyone in the market that too many assets were overpriced. By leaving gold and flooding the world with paper money, the central banks weren't fixing the underlying economic problems, but instead only masking them. The result, as they say, is history: After all of the central banks abandoned gold and flooded their economies with new money—just as Friedman recommended—the world still suffered through many years of economic stagnation.

discount rate occurred only during the 1929–1931 collapse. (In other words, there were no other years in this period that had a rate as high as 7 percent or as low as 1 1/2 percent.) If the "insufficient liquidity" explanation for the 1930s Depression is correct, then the Fed's merciless behavior in 1920–1921 should have spawned a much greater depression, making the 1920s a decade of extreme misery. This is especially true when we consider that the price deflation in 1920–1921 was more extreme than in the early 1930s, so that the "real" interest rate was even more amplified. But as we know, the 1920s were arguably the most prosperous decade in U.S. history.

Really the monetarist explanation is backwards. Tightening the money supply—and other austerity measures, such as cutting government spending—may intensify the short-term pain, but by speeding the liquidation process they hasten the transition to a true recovery. The way out of our current economic slump is not bailouts, trillion dollar "stimulus packages," and Fed handouts of zero-interest-rate loans. These feel-good measures don't provide the proverbial soft landing, but instead prevent the market economy from healing itself.

Milton Friedman and Anna Schwartz's *A Monetary History of the United States* documents the bureaucratic infighting and at times shocking incompetence of the human beings who were running the Federal Reserve during the late 1920s and early 1930s. Their justly praised work is a welcome antidote to the all-too-common tendency to assume that "the authorities" know what they are doing, and that if a new government agency is created to Fix Problem X (such as deflationary bank panics), then that agency can only improve upon what the private sector accomplishes. Notwithstanding its contributions, however, their work created a myth, namely that the Federal Reserve sat idly back and allowed the economy to implode. That myth—like the myth that Herbert Hoover sat idly back and watched the Depression unfold—is continuing to drive misguided policies today.

Chapter 4

DID CONSERVATIVE ECONOMIC POLICIES CAUSE THE DEPRESSION?

mong the popular "lessons" of the Great Depression, liberal critics inform us that the greed of the Roaring '20s made the Depression of the '30s inevitable—a karmic payback for the nation's avarice. And then, once the Depression had set in, President Herbert Hoover allegedly made things worse by stubbornly clinging to the gold standard, an obsolete system that may have served a purpose in the nineteenth century but served only to tie central bankers' hands in the twentieth.

As with the other fables surrounding the Great Depression, these too are myths. The conservative fiscal policies of the Coolidge Administration—spearheaded by Treasury Secretary Andrew Mellon—unleashed entrepreneurs to provide arguably the most prosperous decade in American history. In one sense, the "excesses" of the 1920s did indeed cause the stock market crash, but this was the fault of the Fed's easy-money policies, which can hardly be the fault of laissez-faire capitalism.

Herbert Hoover was right to insist on honoring the dollar's traditional tie to gold at $20.67 an ounce. The classical gold standard of the nineteenth century had truly ushered in a golden era of international commerce and peace. When most belligerents in World War I abandoned gold—in order to use the printing press to pay for the conflict—massive trade distortions

Guess What?

- The government ran a budget surplus every year of the 1920s

- Andrew Mellon cut taxes on the poor

- The gold standard protected citizens from currency debasement

A Few Words from Silent Cal

Calvin Coolidge had a reputation for brevity, but he outdid himself when reelected as president of the Massachusetts state Senate and he gave the following inaugural—reproduced in its entirety:

"Conserve the firm foundations of our institutions. Do your work with the spirit of a soldier in the public service. Be loyal to the Commonwealth, and to yourselves. And be brief—above all things, be brief."

Paul Johnson, *A History of the American People* (New York: Harper Perennial, 1999), 715-16.

began to develop among the nations. Though the major governments gradually pegged their currencies back to gold throughout the 1920s, the "failure" of the gold standard in the 1930s was really the failure of a political quick-fix that was a far cry from the original system. First under FDR and then most especially Richard Nixon, the government removed the dollar's link to gold, ushering in inflation.

The Roaring '20s

After the sharp depression at the beginning of the decade following the First World War, the period from 1923 to 1929 was one of unrivaled prosperity. In this age of relatively limited government, real income *per person* rose 2.1 percent annually, even though the U.S. population increased from 111.9 million to 121.8 million people. Manufacturing output rose 23.5 percent over the whole period, while output per man-hour increased almost 14 percent.[1]

Such statistics cast doubt on the picture of the brutal, wildcat economy you find painted in many American history classes. Still, the proponents of the stereotype could retort, "Sure, unregulated markets create wealth, but it all went to the rich! Your 'average' figures don't capture that."

Yet even this move fails, because the era before government "fine tuning" of the macroeconomy showered unprecedented luxury on the common man. In a market economy, the way to riches is to sell products for *the masses*, since that's where all the money is. Gifted entrepreneurs made fantastic fortunes, to be sure, but—when done in the private sector—only by delivering better products at lower prices to average Americans. Two of the key developments in this period were the delivery of electricity to the masses and the constantly falling price of automobiles. Gene Smiley describes the remarkable 1920s:

> The American economy did not simply produce more of the same things—it produced many new products and services. A key to much of this growth was the spreading use of commercially generated electricity. Electricity was the basis for a great many other new consumer products such as refrigerators, phonographs, electric irons, electric fans, electric lighting, toasters, vacuum cleaners, and other household appliances....Radios and radio stations first appeared in the early twenties and quickly became an important source of news and entertainment as they began to break the isolation of rural life....
>
> Rising incomes and slowly declining workweeks, along with the convenience of the automobile, led to a revolution in leisure activities....More people began to travel regularly, and motor hotels (or motels) and roadside diners that catered to the motoring crowd became common....Cities had to post policemen to direct traffic at intersections and finally began to install electric traffic signals to regulate the crush of city traffic. Suburbs sprang up around cities as the automobile allowed greater ease and flexibility in getting to work....Sears, Roebuck and Montgomery Ward, the two largest mail order (or catalog) firms, opened

Wisdom from Silent Cal

PIG

"Economy is idealism in its most practical form."

Paul Johnson, *A History of the American People*, 716.

retail stores on major streets leading to the downtown areas of cities....[2]

So what spawned this burst in innovation and production? One major factor was the huge tax cuts pushed through by Andrew Mellon. As Treasury Secretary for Harding, Coolidge, and Hoover (for most of his term), Mellon was in charge of the federal government's finances from 1921 through 1932. As such, he plays a large role in our story.

Andrew Mellon's Incredible Tax Cuts

During World War I, the U.S. government ran massive deficits, increasing the federal debt from $1.2 billion in 1916 to a whopping $25.5 billion

Quite a Match: Calvin Coolidge and Andrew Mellon

Although originally tapped as Treasury Secretary for Warren Harding, Andrew Mellon's conservative fiscal policies resonated well with Coolidge's philosophy of limited government. In Coolidge's words: "Government cannot relieve from toil. The normal must take care of themselves. Self-government means self-support....Ultimately, property rights and personal rights are the same thing....History reveals no civilized people among whom there was not a highly educated class and large aggregations of wealth. Large profits mean large payrolls. Inspiration has always come from above."

Paul Johnson, *A History of the American People*, 716.

just three years later (and this was when $25 billion meant something).[3] A very successful banker by trade—he was one of the richest men in America in the 1920s—Mellon assumed his new post with the goal of cleaning up the government's fiscal house. Rather than proposing drastic tax hikes, Mellon called for the opposite strategy.

Anticipating the Laffer Curve and Reagan Revolution by half a century, Mellon thought the key to paying down the federal debt was

Wisdom from Silent Cal

"One of the greatest favors that can be bestowed upon the American people, is economy in government."

Calvin Coolidge 1924 presidential address.

to sharply reduce the crippling tax burdens that had been levied during the war. With lower rates of taxation, the most productive members of society would have the incentive to earn more income, rather than hunkering down and shielding their wealth in tax-exempt instruments such as municipal bonds. As Mellon put it in 1924: "The history of taxation shows that taxes which are inherently excessive are not paid. The high rates inevitably put pressure upon the taxpayer to withdraw his capital from productive business."[4]

Mellon's cuts were quite large. In 1921 the top income earners paid a stifling 73 cents to Washington for every additional dollar they earned. The next year the rate was slashed to 58 percent, and was cut every year thereafter down to 25 percent in 1925, where it remained until the Hoover Administration. The tax burden on poorer citizens was reduced as well, with the lowest bracket's rate being cut from 4 percent in 1921 down to 1.5 percent by 1925. The table below compares the tax brackets from 1921, when Harding assumed office and appointed Mellon, and from 1926, after Mellon's proposed cuts had all been implemented:

Federal Tax Schedule 1921

Married Filing Jointly
Marginal Tax Brackets

Tax Rate	Over	But Not Over
4.0%	$0	$4,000
8.0%	$4,000	$5,000
9.0%	$5,000	$6,000
10.0%	$6,000	$8,000
11.0%	$8,000	$10,000
12.0%	$10,000	$12,000
13.0%	$12,000	$14,000
14.0%	$14,000	$16,000
15.0%	$16,000	$18,000
16.0%	$18,000	$20,000
17.0%	$20,000	$22,000
18.0%	$22,000	$24,000
19.0%	$24,000	$26,000
20.0%	$26,000	$28,000
21.0%	$28,000	$30,000
22.0%	$30,000	$32,000
23.0%	$32,000	$34,000
24.0%	$34,000	$36,000
25.0%	$36,000	$38,000
26.0%	$38,000	$40,000
27.0%	$40,000	$42,000
28.0%	$42,000	$44,000
29.0%	$44,000	$46,000
30.0%	$46,000	$48,000
31.0%	$48,000	$50,000
32.0%	$50,000	$52,000
33.0%	$52,000	$54,000
34.0%	$54,000	$56,000
35.0%	$56,000	$58,000
36.0%	$58,000	$60,000
37.0%	$60,000	$62,000
38.0%	$62,000	$64,000

Federal Tax Schedule 1926

Married Filing Jointly
Marginal Tax Brackets

Tax Rate	Over	But Not
1.5%	$0	$4,000
3.0%	$4,000	$8,000
5.0%	$8,000	$10,000
6.0%	$10,000	$14,000
7.0%	$14,000	$16,000
8.0%	$16,000	$18,000
9.0%	$18,000	$20,000
10.0%	$20,000	$22,000
11.0%	$22,000	$24,000
12.0%	$24,000	$28,000
5.1%	$28,000	$32,000
14.0%	$32,000	$36,000
15.0%	$36,000	$40,000
16.0%	$40,000	$44,000
17.0%	$44,000	$48,000
18.0%	$48,000	$52,000
19.0%	$52,000	$56,000
20.0%	$56,000	$60,000
21.0%	$60,000	$64,000
22.0%	$64,000	$70,000
23.0%	$70,000	$80,000
24.0%	$80,000	$100,000
25.0%	$100,000	

Federal Tax Schedule 1921
(continued)
Married Filing Jointly
Marginal Tax Brackets

Tax Rate Over	Over	But Not Over
39.0%	$64,000	$66,000
40.0%	$66,000	$68,000
41.0%	$68,000	$70,000
42.0%	$70,000	$72,000
43.0%	$72,000	$74,000
44.0%	$74,000	$76,000
45.0%	$76,000	$78,000
46.0%	$78,000	$80,000
47.0%	$80,000	$82,000
48.0%	$82,000	$84,000
49.0%	$84,000	$86,000
50.0%	$86,000	$88,000
51.0%	$88,000	$90,000
52.0%	$90,000	$92,000
53.0%	$92,000	$94,000
54.0%	$94,000	$96,000
55.0%	$96,000	$98,000
56.0%	$98,000	$100,000
60.0%	$100,000	$200,000
64.0%	$150,000	$200,000
68.0%	$200,000	$300,000
71.0%	$300,000	$500,000
72.0%	$500,000	$1,000,000
73.0%	$1,000,000	

Federal Tax Schedule 1926
(continued)
Married Filing Jointly
Marginal Tax Brackets

Tax Rate	Over	But Not

Source: Tax Foundation

Readers familiar with modern Democratic rhetoric might think that Mellon's huge "giveaways to the rich" left gaping holes in the budget. On the contrary, income tax receipts actually increased over the decade, especially during the last few years. And unlike the Reagan years—when the growth in federal receipts was offset by even greater increases in spending—the federal government really did pay down a significant

A Pretty Picture of the Gold Standard Era

"What an extraordinary episode in the economic progress of man that age was which came to an end in August 1914! ... The inhabitant of London could order by telephone, sipping his morning tea in bed, the various products of the whole earth, in such quantity as he might see fit, and reasonably expect their early delivery upon his doorstep; he could at the same moment and by the same means adventure his wealth in the natural resources and new enterprises of any quarter of the world, and share, without exertion or even trouble, in their prospective fruits and advantages; or he could decide to couple the security of his fortunes with the good faith of the townspeople of any substantial municipality in any continent that fancy or information might recommend. He could secure forthwith, if he wished it, cheap and comfortable means of transit to any country or climate without passport or other formality, could despatch his servant to the neighbouring office of a bank for such supply of the precious metals as might seem convenient, and could then proceed abroad to foreign quarters, without knowledge of their religion, language, or customs, bearing coined wealth upon his person, and would consider himself greatly aggrieved and much surprised at the least interference. But, most important of all, he regarded this state of affairs as normal, certain, and permanent, except in the direction of further improvement, and any deviation from it as aberrant, scandalous, and avoidable."

—**John Maynard Keynes**, 1919

amount of its debt, which fell from $24 billion in 1920 to about $17 billion in 1929. In fact, Uncle Sam ran a surplus in every year of the 1920s. Despite the booming prosperity, the federal budget was significantly lower at the end of the decade than at the start.

By all accounts, the 1920s was a period of immense prosperity for the United States. The evidence suggests that one of the primary factors in this success was Andrew Mellon's decision to get the government off the backs of America's entrepreneurs.

Was the Depression Payback for the 1920s Boom?

Anti-capitalist moralizers try to dismiss the prosperity of the 1920s as illusory, and blame the stock market crash and ensuing Depression on this earlier "decade of greed." In his very popular history of the stock market crash, liberal economist John Kenneth Galbraith argues that wild ups and downs are inherent to the nature of unregulated capitalism.[5] But the critics never really explain why letting American producers and workers keep more of their own money is somehow destabilizing. Nor do they explain why Coolidge's budget cuts and debt reduction were examples of profligacy.

A speculative fever swept the country in the latter half of the decade; there is no doubt about that. But many economists argue that the cause was the Federal Reserve's low interest rates. In particular, in 1927 the Fed consciously decided to ease rates (which had the effect of increasing the supply of dollars) in order to take the pressure off the Bank of England.

Wisdom from Silent Cal

"Nine-tenths of a president's callers at the White House want something they ought not to have. If you keep dead still they will run out in three or four minutes."

Paul Johnson, *A History of the American People*, 716.

What had happened was that Great Britain severed the pound's link to gold during World War I, in order to run its printing press to help pay for the war. Naturally, prices in Britain rose because of this inflation in the money supply. But during the 1920s Britain wanted to return to the gold standard at the pre-war parity, of 4.25 pounds sterling to an ounce of gold. Since all along the dollar had been tied to gold at $20.67 an ounce, this implied a dollar/sterling exchange rate of $4.86 to the pound.

The problem was that the free market exchange rate was lower, because the British had inflated more than the Americans had during the war. The British pound was no longer worth $4.86, even though the Bank of England declared otherwise. The inevitable result was a drain of the Bank's gold reserves into American hands. It was this trend that led the British to plead with Federal Reserve officials in 1927 to boost American inflation. The upswing in the Wall Street boom at this time suggests that the Fed's loose policies played a large part in the later crash of 1929.

A contemporary economist who endorsed this theory was the celebrated Lionel Robbins. In his 1934 book on the Great Depression, Robbins quotes from the 1931 testimony of "Mr. A. C. Miller, the most experienced member of the Federal Reserve Board, before the Senate Committee on Banking and Currency," who told the senators:

> In the year 1927... you will note the pronounced increase in these holdings [Federal Reserve holdings of United States securities] in the second half of the year. Coupled with the heavy purchases of acceptances it was the greatest and boldest operation ever undertaken by the Federal Reserve System, and, in my judgment, resulted in one of the most costly errors committed by it or any other banking system in the last 75 years!...
>
> What was the object of Federal Reserve Policy in 1927? It was to bring down money rates, the call rate [the interest rate on loans to "margin buyers" who buy securities with borrowed

When Money Was *Literally* Backed by Gold

Before their confiscation by Roosevelt in 1933, gold certificates circulated as paper currency in the United States. They were similar in some respects to the Federal Reserve Notes of today, but were different in crucial respects. For example, the $50 bill still had a picture of Grant, and it still had a "50" in each of the four corners. But stamped under Grant's picture was the following: "FIFTY DOLLARS IN GOLD COIN PAYABLE TO

THE BEARER ON DEMAND." In addition, the back of the note was literally printed in yellow.

capital] among them, because of the international importance the call rate had come to acquire. The purpose was to start an outflow of gold—to reverse the previous inflow of gold into this country.[6]

How Did the Classical Gold Standard Work?

Many critics of the "obsolete" gold standard don't understand where it came from. They don't realize that the only reason Americans were using green pieces of paper when FDR "mercifully" abandoned gold was that the U.S. government had historically assured them that the dollar was "as good as gold." Herbert Hoover's adherence to the gold standard, then, was—among other things—a simple example of someone keeping his word.

One of the traditional functions of governments has been to issue currency, and paper money was, traditionally, given value by being redeemable for a commodity like silver or gold. (The very term "pound sterling" for the British currency suggests a weight of silver.) Although governments would often renege on their pledges—especially during wars—it is important to realize that the various currencies (like the pound, dollar, or mark) were not "worth" a particular weight in gold or silver, but rather were *defined* as such. For example, when the United States abandoned the bimetallic system (using silver and gold as the monetary standard) and formally went on a gold standard in 1900, it *defined* one U.S. dollar as 23.22 grains (1.505 grams) of gold. The government's role in regulating money was perceived as a matter of establishing uniform weights and measures; a dollar *was* 23.22 grains of gold, the same way that one foot *was* 12 inches. The point wasn't to steer the macroeconomy or create jobs, the point was to provide a uniform standard for citizens to use in their transactions.

Books You're Not Supposed to Read

The Case Against the Fed, Murray N. Rothbard (Auburn, AL: The Ludwig von Mises Institute, 2007)

What Has Government Done to Our Money? Murray N. Rothbard (Auburn, AL: The Ludwig von Mises Institute, 2008)

The Creature from Jekyll Island: A Second Look at the Federal Reserve, G. Edward Griffin (American Media, 2002)

Throughout the nineteenth century, more and more of the major trading countries of the world followed Great Britain's example and tied their currencies to gold. The definitions they adopted then implied corresponding, fixed exchange rates between the various currencies. For example, the U.S. dollar was defined as $20.67 to one troy ounce (31.1 grams) of gold, while the British pound was defined as 4.25 pounds to a gold ounce. Thus, many authors write that under the classical gold standard, the British pound had a fixed exchange rate of $4.86 (some round up to $4.87).

In actual practice, the British pound didn't *literally* always trade for exactly $4.86. After all, unlike inches and feet—which were just different units of length—an ounce of gold and a dollar (or pound) were units of different things. What would happen is that the dollar-price of a British pound (or the pound-price of a U.S. dollar) would be set on international currency markets, with "floating" exchange rates, just as they are set in today's markets. The crucial difference, however, was that the British and American governments were obligated to redeem any amounts of currency presented to them according to the stipulated weights in gold (less a small commission). This set a tight band—centered on $4.86—within which the dollar/pound exchange rate would fluctuate.

It is important to remember that ultimately, the vast majority of people in a given country must be paid in their own currencies. If an American shopkeeper in 1910 wanted to import British tea, he (or someone acting on his behalf) would first need to obtain British pounds. On the other hand, if a British librarian wanted to import back-issues of *The Poor Farmer's Almanac*, she (or her agent) would first need to use British pounds to buy American dollars. The trades would occur in the currency markets, where supply and demand would set the price (exchange rate) between each pair of currencies. If Americans wanted to spend more dollars on British goods and assets than the British wished to spend on American items—when valued at the prevailing exchange rate—then the "surplus" dollars chasing British pounds in the currency markets would push up the dollar-price of a pound, perhaps to $4.88.

However, under the gold standard there was an upper bound on the dollar-price of a British pound. If the American trade deficit[7] continued to grow, eventually the dollar would fall (meaning the dollar-price of a pound would rise) until it reached the "gold export point" (which would depend on shipping and other transactions costs involving gold). To give an extreme example, if the dollar depreciated to $10 per pound, then owners of gold could make a killing. They could sell an ounce of gold in

England at 4.25 pounds (the legally defined value of the pound). Then they could enter the currency markets and receive 42.5 American dollars for the 4.25 pounds (because of our assumed $10 exchange rate). Then they could present the $42.50 in U.S. currency to the United States Treasury, and demand the legally defined payment of roughly 2.06 ounces of gold (because one ounce of gold was defined as $20.67). Thus, absent shipping and other costs, the gold owners would be able to more than double their gold holdings through this arbitrage action.

As with other opportunities for (almost) pure profit in the marketplace, the $10 British pound in our hypothetical scenario would soon correct itself. The transfer of gold from America would force the Fed to reduce the money supply in the U.S. and allow the Bank of England to raise it in England. This would cause domestic prices (measured in dollars) to fall in America, while domestic prices (measured in pounds) would rise in England. The change in domestic prices in the two countries would reverse the trade imbalance, as consumers in both countries tried to buy less from British producers and more from American producers. At the exchange rate of $10 per pound, there would now be more pounds chasing dollars, and so the rate would fall back towards the $4.86 anchor point. Gold would continue to drain out of American vaults and into British ones until the exchange value of the dollar had appreciated back above the gold-export point.

Did the Gold Standard Cause the Depression?

In short, the answer is no, as we pointed out in a sidebar earlier. But the myth is so pernicious that it deserves a fuller explication here.

Conservatives were, traditionally, the supporters of "sound money," because it was a check against inflation, and corrected trade balances. But many liberals have tried to argue that because the gold standard placed handcuffs on the expansionist tendencies of central banks—expansionism they believe was needed to "stimulate" the economy—it caused, or at least greatly exacerbated, the economic hardships of the early 1930s. The smoking gun for this line of argument is the Federal Reserve's decision to reverse its "stimulus" following the stock market crash, by sharply hiking interest rates in 1931 shortly after Great Britain (again) abandoned gold. Fearing that the United States would soon follow, investors around the world presented their dollars for gold. Many critics argue that the United States at this point should have followed the example of Britain and other countries mired in the Depression, and abandon gold too.

But the critics of the gold standard miss the big picture. For one thing, after World War I the various governments wanted to return to gold because the stability it brought to currencies encouraged both international trade and domestic investment.

We should also remember that when governments "went off gold," they were reneging on legal pledges to investors holding their currencies. When governments violate contracts, it creates a lack of trust that discourages investment.

In truth, it is silly to blame "the gold standard" for the Great Depression, since the world never really returned to the classical system after wrecking it in World War I. What governments adopted in its place was

Hoard All You Want, We'll Dig More

From the end of 1925 to the end of 1930, "the monetary gold reserves of the world as a whole increased at a rate of between 2 1/2 and 3 per cent per annum. Even if the theory on which the explanation of the slump in terms of absolute gold shortage is based were correct, it would be inapplicable because it fails to fit the facts. The assertion of a gold shortage is unfounded."

—**Lionel Robbins**, 1934

Lionel Robbins, *The Great Depression* (Auburn, AL: The Ludwig von Mises Institute, 2007 [1934]), 22.

a "gold exchange standard," which did not contain the safeguards of the real McCoy. Murray Rothbard explains the world monetary system as it evolved during the 1920s, and how it invited the later crisis:

> The United States remained on the classical gold standard, redeeming dollars in gold. Britain and the other countries of the West, however, returned to a pseudo-gold standard, Britain in 1926 and the other countries around the same time. British pounds and other currencies were not payable in gold coins, but only in large-sized bars, suitable only for international transactions. This prevented the ordinary citizens of Britain and other European countries from using gold in their daily life, and thus permitted a wider degree of paper and bank inflation. But furthermore, Britain redeemed pounds not merely in gold, but also in dollars; while the other countries redeemed their currencies not in gold, but in pounds. And most of these countries were induced by Britain to return to gold at overvalued parities. The result was a pyramiding of United States [dollars] on gold, of British pounds on dollars, and of other European currencies on pounds—the "gold-exchange standard," with the dollar and the pound as the two "key currencies."

> Now when Britain inflated, and experienced a deficit in its balance of payments, the gold standard mechanism did not work to quickly restrict British inflation. For instead of other countries redeeming their pounds for gold, they kept the pounds and inflated on top of them. Hence Britain and Europe were permitted to inflate unchecked, and British deficits could pile up unrestrained by the market discipline of the gold standard. As for the United States, Britain was able to induce the

United States to inflate dollars [in 1927] so as not to lose many dollar reserves or gold to the United States.

The point of the gold-exchange standard is that it cannot last; the piper must eventually be paid, but only in a disastrous reaction to the lengthy inflationary boom. As sterling balances piled up in France, the United States, and elsewhere, the slightest loss of confidence in the increasingly shaky and jerry-built inflationary structure was bound to lead to general collapse. This is precisely what happened in 1931; the failure of inflated banks throughout Europe, and the attempt of "hard money" France to cash in its sterling balances for gold, led Britain to go off the gold standard completely. Britain was soon followed by the other countries of Europe.[8]

The Final Verdict on Gold

It is worth mentioning that the greatest economic catastrophe the modern world has known occurred only *after* countries abandoned gold during World War I, an event that caused dislocations in trade and production that lingered through the 1930s. Even factoring in the occasional financial "panics," the period of the classical gold standard in the nineteenth and early twentieth centuries was characterized by strong, stable economic growth. Under the classical gold standard, there was nothing like the massive price inflations during the First World War—let alone the German hyperinflation in the 1920s—or the decade-long slump of the Great Depression.

In the United States, gold had been faithfully pegged at $20.67 an ounce from the 1870s until Roosevelt took the United States off the gold standard in 1933.[9] Following World War II, the Bretton Woods monetary agreement installed a new "gold exchange standard," in which the various countries could still redeem dollars for gold, but American citizens could not. Finally, in 1971 Richard Nixon severed the link to gold completely, rendering the dollar a true "fiat" currency, with only the discretion of the Federal Reserve to protect its purchasing power. The following chart shows the history of gold prices, and the relative trustworthiness of the gold standard versus Fed chairmen.

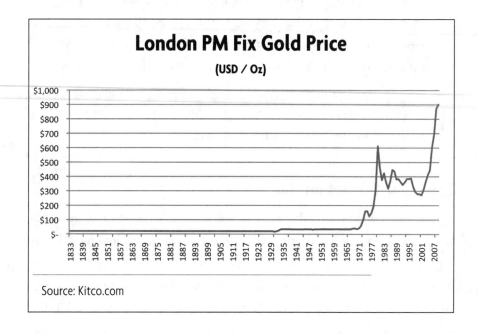

London PM Fix Gold Price
(USD / Oz)

Source: Kitco.com

Chapter 5

THE FAILURES OF THE NEW DEAL

f all the myths of the Great Depression, the one that's most demonstrably false is that the New Deal "got us out of it." Using any measure one likes, the economy was still very weak into the 1940s, meaning that the New Deal did not succeed even after being given seven full years to work its magic. The most immediate indicator of economic health is the unemployment rate, summarized in the following table. Looking at these figures—and recalling that FDR's celebrated "100 days" began in March 1933—one wonders: How in the *world* did historians manage to teach generations of children that the New Deal ended the Depression?

Guess What?

◆ By any measure, the New Deal did not get us out of the Depression

◆ Unemployment remained in double digits until World War II

◆ The New Deal created domestic cartels that drove up prices and drove down employment

◆ Businessmen feared FDR would become a dictator

Period	Average Unemployment Rate
1923–1929	3.3%
1930	8.9
1931	15.9
1932	23.6
1933	24.9
1934	21.7
1935	20.1
1936	17.0
1937	14.3

1938	19.0
1939	17.2
1940	14.6
1941	9.9

Source: Bureau of Labor Statistics[1]

The FDR apologist naturally has a ready reply to the horrific numbers in the table above. Indeed, University of California historian Eric Rauchway argues, "Excepting 1937–1938, unemployment fell each year of Roosevelt's first two terms [while] the U.S. economy grew at average annual growth rates of 9 percent to 10 percent."[2]

This defense of FDR relies on the crudest of logical fallacies. Just because something happened during a particular leader's tenure, doesn't mean that he should be given credit for it. Rather, the correct thing to do is imagine what would have happened if alternate policies had been adopted, and then compare those (speculative) results with the ones that actually occurred. Rauchway's defense of Roosevelt is akin to an Ameri-

New Deal Holy Rollers

"There never has been in American politics a religion so expansively and luminously righteous as the New Deal. From the beginning to the end it was constant in one heroic enterprise—war to the death upon evil, upon greed, poverty and oppression. It had, in fact, one monstrous enemy against which it tilted its shining spear seven days a week and that was SIN. If you criticized the New Deal, you were *for* sin."

—**John T. Flynn**

John T. Flynn, *The Roosevelt Myth* (San Francisco: Fox & Wilkes, 1998), 168.

can military historian crediting Emperor Hirohito for "getting us out of World War II."

Throughout all of economic history, *every* slump eventually ends. *Every* time unemployment rates reach unusual highs, they always come back down—that's why the earlier levels were called "high." Generally speaking, most depressions (or "recessions" as they came to be redefined after the New Deal) in U.S. history were over within two years, and all of them within five. The question that professional economists seek to answer, then, is not, "Exactly how did FDR pull us out of the Depression?" but rather, "Why did the Depression last so long?"

When Roosevelt took office, the unemployment rate was at its highest level in history, and so it's not surprising that the rate tended to fall on his watch—except of course for that little hiccup where it jumped back up to the somewhat disconcerting level of 19 percent, five full years after the New Deal had begun.

Remember that during the severe depression following World War I, unemployment peaked at 11.7 percent in 1921, but was down to 2.4 percent by 1923. Thus, the recovery

I Can't Imagine Why Some Feared Socialism Under FDR . . .

"I personally have long been convinced that the outright ownership of farms ought to be greatly restricted. . . . My own view [is] that under intelligent state control it should be possible to introduce a planned flexibility into the congestion and rigidity of our outdated economic system."

—Undersecretary of Agriculture **Rexford Tugwell**, 1935

Burton Folsom, Jr., *New Deal or Raw Deal? How FDR's Legacy Has Damaged America* (New York: Threshold Editions, 2008), 69.

from that earlier depression witnessed an average yearly drop of more than 4.5 percentage points in the unemployment rate. Had FDR had the same success in battling depression as Warren Harding, the unemployment rate in 1935 would have been 16 percent, rather than above 20 percent as it was under Roosevelt.

Rauchway's observation concerning economic growth is similarly misleading. From 1929 to 1933, real GDP fell an astonishing 27 percent.[3] But any economist could have predicted or expected that after Roosevelt's inauguration there would be a few years of large percentage gains as the economy returned to normal. To give some perspective, the economy grew a little less than 3.5 percent annually during the period from 1900 to 1929, and at more than 4 percent during the 1950s. If these average rates of growth were achieved during periods of relatively full employment, one would expect much larger figures during a period in which a fourth of the labor force had started out on the sidelines. Indeed, UCLA economists Lee E. Ohanian and Harold Cole have published formal models, with all the modern bells and whistles, in top journals arguing that by 1939, total output was still 27 percent below its "trend" value established before the onset of the Depression. They find that investment was even worse, coming in just under 50 percent of where it should have been, had the New Deal truly gotten the economy out of the Depression.[4]

The plain fact is the economy recuperated far more slowly under FDR than it did in any other slump, before or since, in American history. Still, advocates of the New Deal could say that Roosevelt inherited a crisis unlike any in American history. FDR hagiographer William Leuchtenburg writes, "The havoc that had been

The Supreme Court vs. the New Deal

"The mayor of New York City said, 'You cannot leave the destinies of the American people in the hands of a tribunal, no matter how well meaning they may be.' In what hands they should be left, he did not say. But the tribunal to which he was referring [the Supreme Court in its striking down of New Deal legislation] ...said the destinies of the American people should be left in the hands of the American people, and it said this because it is so written in the Constitution."

—**Garet Garrett**, 1935

Salvos Against the New Deal: Selections from the Saturday Evening Post 1933-1940, ed. Bruce Ramsey (U.S.A.: Caxton Press, 2002), 119.

done before Roosevelt took office was so great that even the unprecedented measures of the New Deal did not suffice to repair the damage."[5]

There is just one problem with this thesis: other countries in the 1930s were hit by the Great Depression as well—it was a worldwide collapse, after all—and yet they recovered more quickly than the United States. An excellent illustration of this is the divergence in unemployment rates between the U.S. and its neighbor to the north. Perhaps more than any other single piece of evidence, the following table should dispel the myth of Roosevelt as savior of capitalism.

Period	U.S. Unemployment	Canadian Unemployment
1923–1929	3.3%	3.1%
1930	8.9	9.1
1931	15.9	11.6
1932	23.6	17.6
1933	24.9	19.3
1934	21.7	14.5
1935	20.1	14.2
1936	17.0	12.8
1937	14.3	9.1
1938	19.0	11.4
1939	17.2	11.4
1940	14.6	9.2
1941	9.9	4.4

Sources: Bureau of Labor Statistics, Statistics Canada[6]

The table above is important for several reasons. It reminds us that the Great Depression was not a singularly U.S. experience. Although the Canadian economy did not suffer to the same extent, its downturn was quite severe in its own right. The table also allows us to assess more fairly the potency of the New Deal, because the fortunes of the U.S. and Canadian economies were clearly tied together. Quick calculations reveal, however, that the average gap between U.S. and Canadian unemployment increased under FDR. During the Hoover years (1930 to 1933), American unemployment was, on average, 3.9 points higher than Canada's unemployment. Yet during the (peacetime) heyday of the New Deal from 1934 to 1941, U.S. unemployment, on average, was 5.9 points higher than Canada's. Thus, if one tries to excuse the lingering unemployment of the 1930s on "external shocks" outside of Roosevelt's control, we must nonetheless conclude that the Canadian government did a better job handling such shocks. (Incidentally, the Canadians did not institute a "Northern New Deal" during the 1930s.) In 1942, in fact, the famed economist Joseph Schumpeter blamed the New Deal as the only possible explanation "for the fact that the [United States] which had the best chance of recovering quickly was precisely the one to experience the most unsatisfactory recovery."[7]

This Was Before the Laffer Curve

"In July 1941, as he planned his third term, [Roosevelt] suggested to his budget director a proposal for a 99.5 percent tax rate on all income over $100,000. When the budget director was clearly startled by such a request, Roosevelt replied, 'Why not? None of us is ever going to make $100,000 a year.'"

—Historian **Burt Folsom**

Burton Folsom, Jr., *New Deal or Raw Deal?*, 145.

Continuing the Work of Hoover: Restricting Production and Raising Wages

The shocking unemployment rates of the Hoover years were a direct, if unintended consequence of his high-wage policy. Hoover urged businesses to maintain wage rates, even though profits were plummeting and prices in general were dropping. With firms desperately trying to cut costs to stay afloat during the Depression, Hoover insisted that the relative price of labor *increase*. It is no wonder then that this period witnessed the sharpest pullback in demand for workers in American history. FDR continued these policies.

But FDR had an advantage. The severe price deflation under Hoover turned around just as Roosevelt took office. From March 1929 through March 1933, consumer prices fell a cumulative 26 percent, while from March 1933 to March 1937, they rose a cumulative 13 percent.[8] One of the perverse advantages of inflation is that it can balance off government

You Hate What You Don't Understand

"Roosevelt's string of business failures [during the 1920s] did not surprise those who knew him well. One friend, Franklin Lane, Wilson's secretary of interior, concluded, 'Roosevelt knows nothing about finance, but he doesn't *know* he doesn't know.' Therefore, [Roosevelt] tried one scheme after another, pursuing whims not research, always thinking the next idea would be a winner. Henry Wallace, who would become Roosevelt's vice president, liked his boss in politics but not in business. Wallace had published a newspaper in Iowa and knew the patience and tenacity needed to earn a profit. 'I reached the conclusion,' Wallace said after watching Roosevelt in action, '...that I would under no circumstances, ever have any business dealings with him.'"

—Historian **Burt Folsom**

Burton Folsom, Jr., *New Deal or Raw Deal?*, 25.

high-wage policies (as long as these policies aren't indexed to inflation). To that degree, inflation can help cure unemployment.

There were other, natural trends in place that should have aided Roosevelt. Left to its own devices, the economy would have gradually recovered from the distortions of the late 1920s boom, as unsustainable lines were shut down and resources transferred to the solvent firms; moreover worker productivity would naturally increase thanks to advances in technology and managerial efficiency. Roosevelt should have let wages find their natural market level. If he had, then unemployment rates would have fallen rapidly in the first few years of his administration. Over time, rising prices, worker productivity, and increasing profits would have led to the creation of more jobs and market-related increases in wages.

Thinking Big

"History will probably record the National Industrial Recovery Act as the most important and far-reaching legislation ever enacted by the American Congress."

—Franklin Delano Roosevelt

Quoted in Burton Folsom, Jr., *New Deal or Raw Deal?*, 43.

Unfortunately, FDR did not follow this strategy. Like Hoover before him, FDR thought that the Depression was ultimately due to underconsumption. In fact, FDR outdid Hoover in two respects. First, he sought to actually *raise* wage rates (rather than merely put a floor under them), and second, FDR did not rely on mere jawboning as Hoover had done. On the contrary, Roosevelt decided that if the president wanted something done, he ought to use the might of the federal government to force it upon the country. Economists Lee E. Ohanian and Harold Cole explain how the New Deal implemented FDR's vision: "Roosevelt's recipe for economic recovery was raising prices and wages. To achieve these increases, Congress passed industrial and labor policies to limit competition and raise labor bargaining power.... [P]rices and wages rose substantially after these policies were adopted."[9]

One of these policies was the National Industrial Recovery Act (NIRA) (1933–35). This act created the National Recovery Administration (NRA), which provided a vehicle for the major players in each industry to create a so-called "Code of Fair Competition." In reality, these codes were *anti*-competitive rules that forbade industries from lowering prices. In short, the NRA worked by fostering giant cartels, which made products artificially expensive and punished small businesses trying to compete against big businesses. As a condition for being allowed to form such a cartel, Roosevelt insisted that each participating "industry [raise] wages and [accept] collective bargaining with an independent union."[10] By 1934, over 500 industries had adopted such codes, covering almost 80 percent of private, nonfarm employment. With these "voluntary" codes in place, big producers could raise prices without fear of losing market share, because the federal government itself would punish any "unpatriotic" upstarts who dared try to undersell the large firms.

Typical leftists worry that free markets foster monopolies, but history shows the opposite. Roosevelt had to use the power of the federal government to *force* cartels upon American industries. In a free market, big businesses certainly want high prices and little competition, but without government intervention to squash upstart competitors, private-sector cartels just don't work.

Holy New Deal!

"Hugh Johnson, the man Roosevelt put at the head of the NRA, called it a 'Holy Thing…the Greatest Social Advance Since the Days of Jesus Christ.'"

—Historian **Burt Folsom**

Burton Folsom, Jr., *New Deal or Raw Deal?*, 45.

After the Supreme Court threw out the NIRA as unconstitutional in 1935, Roosevelt shifted gears. The National Labor Relations Act (NLRA) achieved his aims via the workers. Rather than allowing large businesses to directly set prices—which the Supreme Court had ruled an unacceptable violation of antitrust laws—the NLRA instead granted unions incredible bargaining power, forcing businesses to accept collective bargaining. The new National Labor Relations Board made sure that businesses accepted the results of their negotiations with the unions. The point was that with high wages guaranteed, businesses would be forced to raise prices. High wage rates, of course, and other restrictive aspects of the law also helped to dampen free market competition just as the NIRA had done.

As a result of the NLRA (also known as the Wagner Act), union membership more than doubled, increasing from 13 percent of the work force in 1935 to 29 percent in 1939, while the number of "strike days" doubled in one year, from 14 million in 1936 to 28 million in 1937.[11] Labor economists point to this incredible surge in union strength—and the high wages it brought—as an important factor in the persistently high unemployment of the 1930s.

Knowing all too well that government programs often have a knack for failing to achieve their stated objectives, Cole and Ohanian studied whether the NIRA and then the NLRA actually had an impact on prices

Bureaucrats Know Best

"A mere builder of more industrial plants, a creator of more railroad systems, an organizer of more corporations, is as likely to be a danger as a help. Our task is not . . . necessarily producing more goods. It is the soberer, less dramatic business of administering resources and plants already in hand."

—**Franklin Delano Roosevelt**

Quoted in Harold L. Cole and Lee E. Ohanian, "New Deal Policies and the Persistence of the Great Depression: A General Equilibrium Analysis," 4.

and wages. In general, such analyses are fraught with difficulties, because it is difficult to know how history would have unfolded under different circumstances. However, Cole and Ohanian discovered the closest thing to a controlled experiment in economics, in the case of the bituminous coal versus the anthracite coal sectors. The firms and workers in bituminous coal were covered by a Code of Fair Competition under the NIRA, but for whatever reason the anthracite coal industry could not reach agreement and remained uncovered. Cole and Ohanian found that the (trend-adjusted real) wages of bituminous coal miners rose sharply from 1933 to 1934, and continued rising throughout the decade, while the wages of anthracite coal miners declined sharply from 1933 to 1934, and then continued to moderately decline every year until 1938. Switching from the workers to the products, Cole and Ohanian found that the relative wholesale price of anthracite coal was flat from 1933 to 1934, and had fallen some 15 percent by the end of the decade. In contrast, the price of bituminous coal—for which an NIRA code had been adopted—increased almost 20 percent from 1933 to 1934 alone, and continued rising until the end of 1935.[12]

Standard economics explains these results. The bituminous coal miners achieved wage increases and other limits on output because they were covered by an NRA code. This led to rising prices for buyers of bituminous coal. On the other hand, the "unprotected" anthracite coal sector received the displaced workers from the high-wage bituminous sector. This pushed down wages, and increased output, in the anthracite industry, leading to lower prices for its customers. The general lesson is that government-sponsored cartels don't help the economy as a whole; at best they help particular groups while hurting others.

Overall, the NIRA and NLRA reduced economic efficiency, because labor and other resources were directed only in part by market price signals, but also in significant part by the vagaries of the political process. The New Deal turned American industries into de facto cartels—becoming, in essence, domestic versions of OPEC—and while that might have

Surprisingly Good Advice from a Brain Truster

"I wish I could convert anybody in Washington to the theory that you cannot run a government based on business and have a perpetual warfare with business at the same time."

—Assistant Secretary of State **Adolf Berle**, 1937

had short-term benefits for unionized workers and bosses of big firms in the cartelized industries, it came at the cost of the country as a whole because it resulted in artificially high prices, artificially high unemployment, and politically allocated—rather than market allocated—capital and labor. So not only did the New Deal keep workers on the sidelines, but it also ensured that many of those who *did* have a job worked in the wrong sectors. By preventing wage cuts and impeding the market's attempts to reshuffle resources after the bust, FDR's policies worked to freeze the economy in its 1933 condition. The top-down planning of the New Deal thus bears a large portion of the blame for America's agonizingly slow recovery from the Depression.

The Only Thing We Have to Fear Is Roosevelt Himself

Why did it take so long for the economy to recover after it hit rock bottom in 1933? Economists might point to the data on private investment. Adjusted for price inflation, private investment did not regain its 1929 level until 1941. In fact, those who controlled private capital largely walked away from the U.S. economy for the entire 1930s, refusing to pump in enough new investment even to replace the machinery and goods-in-process that were consumed during the decade. By this measure, what economists call "net investment," America actually went into the red with investment falling to less than zero for much of the Depression. During the period 1931 to 1935, net investment was negative $18.3 billion, and it once again fell to negative $800 million in 1938.[13]

This "capital strike" was a critical factor in the lackluster recovery, and the inability of the private sector to absorb the giant pool of unemployed workers back into useful niches. In fact, the lack of investment during the period casts into question even the rebounding GDP figures touted by Roosevelt admirers. On the fifth anniversary of the New Deal in 1938, Garet Garrett considered this question in his column for the *Saturday Evening Post*:

> All through the rise in American production, even when it was at the top in 1937, there was a sign of weakness in it. The high

Businessmen Weren't the Only Ones Who Were Alarmed

"Truman had little use for the FBI and its director, J. Edgar Hoover, in contrast to Franklin Roosevelt, who had liked the way Hoover got results and greatly enjoyed the spicy secrets Hoover passed on to him about the private lives of important people. It had been Roosevelt, in 1936, who had quietly ordered Hoover to begin gathering political information, a policy Truman strongly disliked. Truman considered Hoover and the FBI a direct threat to civil liberties, and he made no effort now, as Roosevelt had, to ingratiate himself with Hoover...

"'We want no Gestapo or Secret Police,' Truman wrote in his diary after only a month as President. 'FBI is tending in that direction. They are dabbling in sex-life scandals and plain blackmail. ... *This must stop.*'"

—Truman biographer **David McCullough**

David McCullough, *Truman* (New York: Simon and Schuster, 1992), 367.

output was of such things as the economist calls nondurable goods, meaning the things we make today and consume tomorrow. Of durable goods, meaning such things as machinery, power plants, industrial buildings and houses, the great deficit that had accrued in the depression years 1929–1932 was never made up. This means that in order to reach again the level of 1928 in the production of nondurable goods, we were using very largely the equipment we already had, and wearing it out. As far as we did that, we were eating up our tools. Through five years of recovery, ending suddenly in another depression [in 1938], it is doubtful the total wealth of the country was increased at all.[14]

Yet to blame the slow American recovery on weak investment simply pushes back the problem one step: Why were investors so reluctant to risk their funds in the U.S. economy during the 1930s?

The Keynesian answer, of course, is that businesses won't invest if demand has fallen off for their finished products. Why expand your plant when you're already operating below capacity and piling up inventory? Indeed, this is precisely the answer Paul Krugman gave when George Will raised the issue of (non-)investment during the New Deal on ABC's *This Week*.[15]

The problem with the conventional Keynesian explanation is that it proves too much. In the simplest Keynesian story, every recession ought to lead to mass starvation. After all, their theory is that consumers for some inexplicable reason get spooked and reduce their spending. This causes sales to fall off, so businesses slash prices and lay off workers. The layoffs cause national income to fall, leading to a further decline in aggregate demand. And so on in a downward spiral until half the population die and the rest return to the fields. Krugman's "explanation" for the stagnant investment of the 1930s can't explain why the U.S. economy managed to quickly recover from all of the earlier depressions in its history, and all without the massive deficits he believes were needed to escape the Great Depression. Because his diagnosis doesn't distinguish earlier depressions from the Great One, we have no reason to trust Krugman's prescription.

In contrast to Krugman's theory, Bob Higgs advanced a revolutionary thesis in a 1997 paper that could explain what made the Great Depression different from all previous slumps.[16] Higgs attributed much of investor skittishness to "regime uncertainty":

> [T]he insufficiency of private investment from 1935 through 1940 reflected a pervasive uncertainty among investors about the security of their property rights in their capital and its prospective returns. This uncertainty arose, especially, though not exclusively, from the character of the actions of the federal government and the nature of the Roosevelt administration during the so-called Second New Deal, from 1935 to 1940.[17]

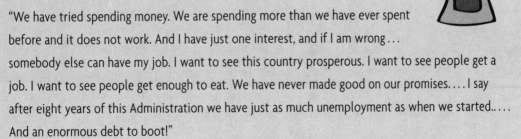

Treasury Secretaries Don't Talk Like that Anymore!

"We have tried spending money. We are spending more than we have ever spent before and it does not work. And I have just one interest, and if I am wrong... somebody else can have my job. I want to see this country prosperous. I want to see people get a job. I want to see people get enough to eat. We have never made good on our promises. . . . I say after eight years of this Administration we have just as much unemployment as when we started.. . . . And an enormous debt to boot!"

—Secretary of the Treasury **Henry Morgenthau, Jr.**, May 1939

Quoted in Burton Folsom, Jr., *New Deal or Raw Deal?*, 2.

Higgs's thesis is entirely plausible. There is a substantial, and growing, body of empirical evidence demonstrating that countries with secure property rights tend to have higher rates of investment and growth than those countries in which the government has wider discretion over the affairs of business.[18] Both opponents and proponents of the New Deal must agree, that among its other features it represented a quantum leap in federal intervention in the economy, and hence an attenuation of private property rights. If it seems straightforward that the free, capitalistic countries of the West prosper because of their institutions of private property, then it naturally follows that the New Deal would sabotage this mechanism.

From our modern vantage point, we recognize the limits the New Deal set on free enterprise, and we can see that the restrictions would have made investment less attractive. But Higgs's point is deeper: it was not simply that the new rules were less profitable, but that the rules themselves kept changing. Businessmen had no hope of guessing which way the New Deal would unfold, because Roosevelt himself didn't know! Burt Folsom explains:

> The New Deal, especially in the area of finance, was rarely the result of consistent planning. As Roosevelt conceded, "We seldom know, six weeks in advance, what we are going to do." Some historians profess to see a first New Deal from 1933 to 1934 and a second New Deal in 1935 and 1936, but Roosevelt, [Felix] Frankfurter, and other New Dealers admitted that most programs were experimental—trial and error. "It is common

---

Land of the Free?

"When [NRA chief] Hugh Johnson was asked what would happen to those 'who won't go along with the new code,' Johnson threatened, 'They'll get a sock in the nose.'"

—Historian **Burt Folsom**

Quoted in Burton Folsom, Jr., *New Deal or Raw Deal?*, 53.

sense," Roosevelt said, "to take a method and try it: If it fails, admit it frankly and try another. But above all, try something."[19]

An anecdote regarding Roosevelt's reneging on gold clauses in government contracts illustrates his complete disregard for business's desire for stability. According to Secretary of the Treasury Henry Morgenthau:

> The President argued with me that he wanted me to keep things on an unsettled basis until the Supreme Court handed down its decision. He said that he wanted this for judicial and political reasons. He said the only way the man in a taxicab can become interested in the gold case is if we kept the story on the front page. He said I want bonds to move up and down and [chaos in] Foreign Exchange. He said if we keep things in a constant turmoil if the case should go against us the man on the street will say for God's sake, Mr. President, do something about it and, he said, if I do everybody in the country will heave a sigh of relief and say thank God.[20]

First They Came for the Businessmen, and I Didn't Speak Up...

"[Businessmen] realize that they are on trial before judges who have the verdict in their pocket beforehand, that an increasing part of public opinion is impervious to their point of view, and that any particular indictment will, if successfully met, at once be replaced by another."

—Joseph Schumpeter, 1939[3]

Quoted in Robert Higgs, *Depression, War, and Cold War* (New York: Oxford University Press, 2006), 12.

With the rules in flux, and the president being advised by some intellectuals who openly questioned the wisdom of capitalism, it is no surprise that private investment did not resume after the trough of the Depression in 1933. Consider the formation of the Securities and Exchange Commission (SEC). Modern Americans take it for granted that this was a wonderful new body that would prevent the "excesses" that had (allegedly) caused the stock market crash, but financial firms at the time certainly did not share this perspective. According to Raymond Moley, Columbia Ph.D., and member of the original "Brain Trust," after the formation of the SEC "the market for new securities was virtually frozen during the year that followed. Bankers and lawyers were unwilling to advise investors to risk entanglement with a law that might be enforced with Draconian severity."[21]

We need to remember that businessmen in the 1930s had plenty of images of strong leaders around the world—Stalin, Mussolini, and Hitler to name a few—and it did not seem beyond possibility at the time that Roosevelt, with the many leftist New Dealers in the administration, might bring socialism to the United States. As Bob Higgs notes in his compelling analysis, "Roosevelt, we now know, never became a dictator along the lines of his contemporaries Stalin, Mussolini, and Hitler; the New Dealers were no Brown Shirts. But what seems so obvious to us in retrospect had quite a different appearance to many contemporaries."[22]

To bolster his case, Higgs draws on surveys of business executives during the New Deal era. For example, Higgs summarizes a *Fortune* poll taken in November 1941 (before Pearl Harbor):

> The question was: "Which of the following comes closest to being your prediction of the kind of economic structure with which this country will emerge after the war?" The respondents were presented with four options, as follows (the per-

I'm Not Sure I Want to Invest Right Now...

"Practices of the unscrupulous money changers stand indicted in the court of public opinion, rejected by the hearts and minds of men....The money changers have fled from their high seats in the temple of our civilization."

—Franklin Delano Roosevelt

centage of respondents selecting that option... is shown in brackets):

(1) A system of free enterprise restored very much along the prewar lines, with modifications to take care of conditions then current [7.2 percent]

(2) An economic system in which government will take over many public services formerly under private management but still leave many opportunities for private enterprise [52.4 percent]

(3) A semi-socialized society in which there will be very little room for the profit system to operate [36.7 percent]

(4) A complete economic dictatorship along fascist or communist lines [3.7 percent][23]

Books You're Not Supposed to Read

Salvos Against the New Deal: Selections from the Saturday Evening Post 1933-1940, Garet Garrett (U.S.A.: Caxton Press, 2002)

New Deal or Raw Deal? How FDR's Legacy Has Damaged America, Burton Folsom, Jr. (New York: Threshold Editions, 2008)

The Roosevelt Myth, John T. Flynn (San Francisco: Fox & Wilkes, 1998)

Clearly, the New Deal fundamentally changed the federal government's role in American society and in doing so created uncertainty among businessmen. When his revolutionary programs were declared unconstitutional in 1935, Roosevelt famously threatened to pack the Supreme Court, a shocking move that made even some of his most stalwart supporters begin to waver. His fiery campaign rhetoric made it clear that Roosevelt was *against* businessmen, blaming them for the economic slump, and considered their subordination a key aim. Finally, regarding the now-humorous worries of dictatorship, the reader should recall that every previous president in American history (except Ulysses S. Grant[24]) had followed George Washington's example by not seeking a third term.

Roosevelt was the first (and only) president to serve more than two terms, and only his death removed him from office. Given the sweep of collectivism across the rest of the world at the time, the attitudes documented by Higgs are quite understandable.

As one last word on the issue of businessmen's fear of FDR, we quote from Roosevelt's speech at Madison Square Garden during his 1936 reelection campaign. After railing against the "economic royalists" and "organized money," Roosevelt thundered:

> Never before in all our history have these forces been so united against one candidate as they stand today. They are unanimous in their hate for me—and I welcome their hatred. I should like to have it said of my first Administration that in it the forces of selfishness and of lust for power met their match. I should like to have it said of my second Administration that in it these forces met their master.[25]

Chapter 6

THE OUTRAGES OF THE NEW DEAL

The New Deal not only failed as an economic recovery program, it was implemented with a menacing force that often goes unremarked. Antiseptic treatments in typical American history textbooks go through the laundry list of New Deal organizations and when they were created, but rarely mention the armed men that knocked malcontents into line.

Roosevelt's "Bank Holiday"

One of Roosevelt's first acts was to shut down the nation's banks. The website History.com provides a typically fawning account of the episode:

> When Franklin Roosevelt started his first term in the White House in 1933, he inherited a nation in the depths of the Depression. A record 13 million Americans were unemployed and businesses were drowning in red ink. Perhaps even more pressing was the head-spinning string of bank failures which had triggered a frantic run on the nation's savings vaults. The wave of withdrawals by panic-stricken depositors further

Guess What?

- Government intervention caused the bank panics of the 1930s
- Roosevelt set the gold price based on "lucky" numbers
- The government paid farmers to destroy food while Americans went hungry
- Roosevelt used WPA money to win elections for Democrats

119

dried up banks' already-depleted supply of liquid assets and pushed the nation's banking system to the brink of disaster. On March 5—the day after being sworn into office—Roosevelt stepped into the breach and declared a "bank holiday," which, for four days forced the closure of the nation's banks and halted all financial transactions. The "holiday" not only helped stem the frantic run on banks, but gave Roosevelt time to push the Emergency Banking Act through the legislative chain. Passed by Congress on March 9, the act handed the president a far-reaching grip over bank dealings and "foreign transactions." The legislation also paved the path for solvent banks to resume business as early as March 10. Three short days later nearly 1,000 banks were up and running again.[1]

This standard depiction of Roosevelt's policy epitomizes the historian's distortion of the nature of the New Deal and its impact on "the little guy." In plain English, let us review exactly what happened: Commercial banks allowed regular Joes and Janes to deposit their life savings with them, and told them: "You can withdraw your money any time you want. This is a *demand* deposit you are making." Then the bankers decided to lend out most of these deposits, rather than storing them in the vault. There are plenty of economists with staunch laissez-faire credentials who do not object to this practice of "fractional reserve" banking,[2] but such practices obviously make banks more vulnerable to bank run panics. (Just as an intellectual exercise, we should recognize that even if banks held 100 percent reserves, they could still turn a profit, the same way that owners of storage units turn a profit without renting 90 percent of their clients' stored furniture.) And even in a fractional reserve banking system, certain safeguards could be put in place. The banks could, for instance, make a formal contractual provision specifying that they had the right to refuse to honor demands for immediate withdrawal (as Jimmy Stewart's savings and loan apparently did in *It's A Wonderful Life*). The system can be self-policing.

But this is not what happened in 1933. If the banks subject to runs had the legal ability to turn their customers away, they didn't need the president of the United States to order it so. When a clerk is locking up a convenience store for the night, she can tell a line of 100 people demanding Slurpies, "Go home, we open tomorrow at 6 a.m." There's nothing mysterious about this.

In this case, major banks had lent out most of their customers' hard-earned savings, boosting the banks' profits and hoping the risky scheme wouldn't blow up in their faces. When it *did* blow up in their faces, and the bankers effectively defaulted on their contractual obligations, the tenderhearted Roosevelt swooped in and unilaterally absolved them of their responsibilities. Then, in an added flourish, Roosevelt also closed every other bank, even ones not subject to runs. The poor sap who needed access to his life savings that week was out of luck, because Roosevelt helped bankers out of the pickle they'd created for themselves.

Besides the dubious morality of siding with the bankers against the legitimate claims of their depositors, there is also the obvious fact that the bank holiday did not magically fix the problems with the U.S. banking system. Then, as today, average investors and depositors were not subject to a sudden bout of irrational anxiety; the crises in the financial sector in the 1930s and in the late 2000s were very real. Roosevelt's euphemistic "holiday" did not change this inconvenient truth, as Jesse Jones of the Reconstruction Finance Corporation explained:

Maybe He Would Have Been Happier with a Private Sector Job?

"[FDR's second-in-command John Nance] Garner deprecated his own office, saying that the vice-presidency was 'not worth a saucer of warm spit.'"

—Historian **Paul Johnson**

A History of the American People (New York: Harper Perennial, 1999), 754.

> It developed that probably no fewer than 5,000 banks required considerable added capital to make them sound.... It could easily be charged, and properly so, that a fraud was practiced on the public when the President proclaimed during the bank holiday [fireside chat] broadcast that only sound banks would be permitted to reopen. It was not until the late spring of 1934, nearly fourteen months afterward, that all the banks doing business could be regarded as solvent.[3]

The usual "lesson" regarding the bank runs is that the noble FDR established the Federal Deposit Insurance Corporation (FDIC) in the Banking Act/Glass-Steagall Act of 1933. Because they no longer feared the loss of their deposits if their bank went belly up, the public now had no reason to rush upon a bank when its health came into doubt.

It is true that the creation of FDIC ended the phenomenon of mass bank runs in the United States. (They still exist in modified form: just ask the hundreds of IndyMac customers who waited in line for more than an hour to get their money after the FDIC closed and then reopened their bank in July 2008.[4]) But this raises an interesting question: Why didn't the banks have *private* insurance to prevent the disasters of the 1930s? After all, the federal government doesn't have entire agencies devoted to insuring, say, commercial trucking fleets and airliners; the companies themselves take out policies with private insurers and pay the premiums. If the FDIC is such a wonderful legacy of the New Deal that rescued the banking system from itself, we have to ask: Why didn't commercial banks take out private insurance for their deposits, just as other firms take out private insurance policies on their business assets?

The answer is what economists call "moral hazard." Certain types of events cannot be insured against, because the very act of providing insurance on them would make them likely to occur. For example, suppose a man called up his insurance broker and said, "I'm planning a trip to

Vegas. I have been there thirty-eight times so far, and usually I make a few bucks. However, on one occasion I really lost my shirt, when I dropped a cool three grand. The wife didn't talk to me for a week after that one, so I would please like a policy protecting me from a catastrophic loss. I'll pay a deductible, let's say $1,000. But after that, you guys pick up the tab. Of course, I'm going to *try* to win—it doesn't help me any to lose a thousand dollars! So what do you say? What premium would you need to charge, to make it worth your while?"

Clearly, no insurance company would entertain the proposal. The man's previous gambling history would be irrelevant, because with an insurance policy he would gamble much more recklessly—especially as he neared his $1,000 "deductible." The company could of course put a cap on the total payout, and perhaps stipulate guidelines for the type of gambling that was covered in the policy, but it is obvious that there would be no mutually advantageous arrangement in this setting. Rather than pay the exorbitant premiums the insurer would need to charge to make it a profitable policy, the man would rather bear the risk himself.

A similar analysis applies to the "insurance" of commercial bank deposits. Banks always had it within their power to guard against a bank run—they could keep 100 percent reserves in the vault, and charge their customers a fee for storage and checking services. But once they deviated from that safe position—by taking some of their clients' deposits and investing them—they exposed themselves to the risk of a bank run, in exchange for the returns on the loans or other investments so acquired. It would be impossible for insurers to write policies against bank runs, because the banks themselves had such a large discretion over their vulnerability.

Through the creation of FDIC, the government has not altered the impracticality of insuring against bank runs. On the contrary, all the government has done is put taxpayers on the hook for potential liabilities that no private insurer would ever dream of assuming. Thus the bankers are free to continue risking their clients' deposits, while the public's last option for keeping them in line—the bank run—has been rendered moot. The FDIC's bailout of the S&L losses of the 1980s ultimately cost taxpayers some $519 billion,[5] and we have yet to learn the costs we'll be paying to bail out the banks in the most recent financial crash.

Besides the risk foisted on taxpayers, the FDIC is insidious because it replaces the safeguards of the market with those provided by one-size-fits-all regulation. Precisely because their customers' deposits (up to a certain threshold) are guaranteed by the taxpayers, banks have the incentive to take riskier positions with the promise of greater payoff. Naturally, when the government created the FDIC it was aware of this and so insisted on further regulation to protect its interests. Instead of banks being relatively free to invest their funds as they saw fit—but being subject to suffering the losses when they made mistakes—the FDIC (and other provisions of the Glass-Steagall Act) socialized the losses and ultimately made D.C. bureaucrats responsible for the integrity of the banking system.

To appreciate the harm of this conversion, we must realize that banks in the early 1930s weren't subject to random runs by their fickle customers. On the contrary, it was those banks that had behaved most recklessly—or even fraudulently—that were the largest "victims" of customers who simply wanted to get their own money back. For example, a 1931 Federal Reserve study of 105 member banks that had failed in that year found, "The principal cause of the failures was poor and dishonest lending practices, particularly 'lax lending methods,' 'slack collection methods,' 'unwise loans to directors and officers,' and 'lack of credit data.'"[6] (Does this sound familiar?)

Some readers might agree that Roosevelt's solution of the bank holiday was imperfect, but nonetheless necessary. "Even if it were true," such readers could think, "that the unmolested market would weed out bad banks, nonetheless the short-term pain of bank panics was intolerable.

Wasn't There a Quote about Absolute Power...?

"[Jesse] Jones called himself, and encouraged others to do so, 'Uncle Jesse.' In turn, it was said of him that he was 'the first financial pirate to realize that the new field of opportunity lay in public service'—hence his unofficial title, the 'Economic Emperor of America.' Jones eventually possessed himself of Hoover's old job as secretary of commerce, and piled up other titles, heading the Federal Loan Administration, the RFC Mortgage Company, the Disaster Loan Corporation, the Federal National Mortgage Corporation, the Export-Import Bank, the Federal Housing Administration, the Census Bureau, the Bureau of Standards, the Civil Aeronautics Board, the Patent Office, the Coast and Geodetic Survey—plus another four important posts he added during World War Two. Never before had one man possessed so much public power in a democratic society."

—Paul Johnson

A History of the American People, 754.

Better to have the certainty, albeit with taxpayer losses, afforded by the FDIC."

There is just one problem with this rationalization: The bank runs were themselves caused by prior government intervention into the banking system. Although third-party insurance was not a feasible private sector solution to bank vulnerability, branch banking was. It is true that the nature of fractional reserve banking allowed any bank chain, no matter how apparently mighty, to be brought to its knees if all of its customers decided to withdraw their funds at once. However, in practice, it was mostly small regional banks that failed during the banking panics of the early 1930s. Jim Powell explains:

Bank customers generally preferred working with a local office, which meant that small-town banks couldn't effectively solicit customers in different regions. When a small-town bank's region—say, the Corn Belt—got in economic trouble, the bank was unlikely to survive. Its principal depositors were corn farmers who went broke and needed to draw down their deposits. Corn farmers were also the principal borrowers and couldn't make the payments on their loans.[7]

Given these realities, one would have expected that most bank offices would be served by large chains, as it were, so that the risk of regional distress could be handled through diversification. But small-town bankers successfully lobbied many state governments for "unit banking laws," which prohibited branch banking. This made the entire U.S. banking system much more vulnerable to the deflationary stresses after the stock market crash. Thousands of U.S. banks failed during the panics of the 1930s, most in states with unit banking laws.

In contrast, Canada allowed branch banking and experienced *zero* bank failures during the Great Depression. According to Milton Friedman and Anna Schwartz, in Canada "10 banks with 3,000-odd branches throughout the country did not even experience any runs," even though Canada experienced the same decline in its quantity of money as the United States did.[8]

There is one final element to the banking panics necessary to put the federal government's "rescue" in perspective. Roosevelt did not come up with the notion of a bank holiday on his own. On the contrary, the various governors had instituted their own statewide holidays, one after the other, throughout 1933, starting with Michigan's eight day "holiday" beginning on February 14. Economic historian Elmus Wicker argues that the governors were causing the very problem they thought they were containing:

> Bank moratoria introduced a new source of depositor uncertainty. . . . The bank holiday was the mechanism for transmit-

ting banking unrest from state to state. The declaration of a banking holiday in one state motivated depositors to withdraw deposits from out-of-state banks to meet their immediate transaction needs thereby transmitting withdrawal pressures to contiguous states and to the New York and Chicago money markets. Moreover, depositors in surrounding states became alarmed that similar deposit restrictions would be imposed in their states and would therefore rush to withdraw deposits in anticipation of a bank moratorium.[9]

The conventional story, in which FDR rescued struggling depositors from a malfunctioning, unregulated banking system, is exactly backward. The banking system was vulnerable in the first place because of (state) government intervention, and the panic was exacerbated by further (state) interference with private transactions. Roosevelt's "solution" did not correct the fundamental problems with the banks, but instead took away bank clients' incentives to monitor bank solvency by saddling taxpayers with any losses.

Going Off Gold

The Emergency Banking Act of 1933, besides declaring the bank holiday, also took the United States off the gold standard. Gene Smiley describes the quick sequence of events:

> The ... Act gave Roosevelt the power to control foreign exchange transactions and gold and currency movements, options that he quickly utilized. On April 5 he issued an executive order requiring American citizens to surrender all gold certificates and gold except for rare gold coins. On April 18 he prohibited the private export of gold and indicated he would support the Thomas Amendment to the Agricultural Adjustment Act, allowing the

president to set the price of gold—an action that clearly meant devaluing the dollar. The dollar then began to float and declined in value against most currencies. On June 5, Congress abrogated all gold clauses in contracts.[10]

Short of herding tens of thousands of children into concentration camps—something Roosevelt also did: remember the Japanese internment camps—it would be difficult for the president to behave in a more tyrannical fashion. The gold certificates held by the public had not been gifts from the U.S. Treasury. On the contrary, they were redemption tickets for which individuals and companies had traded away actual gold, or other goods and services, because the United States government had pledged, since 1873, to surrender physical gold to anyone bearing the certificates, at the rate of $20.67 per ounce. Ordering the public to turn in the gold certificates, in exchange for Federal Reserve Notes (noticeably lacking the key phrase "PAYABLE TO THE BEARER"), was naked theft, just as surely as if President Obama ordered the public to turn in all iPhones in exchange for Blackberries. The theft would be made quite explicit when the government officially tied the dollar back to gold the following year, but at the rate of $35 per troy ounce, a depreciation of more than 40 percent. (Note that American citizens still could not redeem their paper currency for gold at *any* exchange rate.)

Ordering the public to turn over its gold—under penalty of a $10,000 fine and up to ten years in prison[11]—was a clear-cut robbery. At the time of the revaluation of the dollar, the government held some 190 million ounces—almost 6,000 *tons*—of gold.[12] The famous bullion depository at Fort Knox was built precisely to house all of the gold that FDR seized from the American people. Yet insidious as the explicit confiscation was, the cancellation of gold clauses in contracts was in a way a more fundamental violation of property rights. Before Roosevelt's move, many private individuals sought to protect themselves from an unexpected government debasement by putting clauses in their contracts specifying that a party's obligation was to be determined according to a weight of gold, *not* a particular number of U.S. dollars. (So long as the government had maintained the peg at $20.67 per ounce, the gold clause would be redundant.) Thus, for all debtors—including the U.S. government itself—who were obligated contractually to pay gold, the Emergency Banking Act provided a clear windfall, because it voided these contractual "gold clauses" and allowed debtors to pay back in (devalued) dollars.

Yet this is not the truly insidious feature of the new law. The confiscation of gold, and the gift to debtors, in 1933 was a massive crime, but a one-shot event. But even going forward, private individuals were not allowed to insist on payments tied to gold. (Gold clauses were once again legalized in 1977.) This continued prohibition on gold clauses is significant, and reflects the ultimate objectives of the government. After adjusting to the confiscation, the private sector might still have retained the benefits of a market-based, commodity money, by defining contractual obligations in terms of the price of gold as it was determined in the world market. In this way investors could have removed some of the uncertainty of further debasement of the dollar, by locking in a contractual peg to gold. Yet the government courts would not enforce such contracts, and so the private sector had no choice but to use unbacked green pieces of paper as the foundation of its transactions. Americans were now entirely at the mercy of those controlling the printing press.

Before leaving this episode, we should address one possible objection to the harsh criticism leveled above. Even if it were true that the government in a sense robbed the public, isn't that a particularly cynical way of viewing the matter? If Roosevelt really believed—as he said during his fireside chats—that gold hoarding was exacerbating the Depression, then shouldn't we at worst criticize his economic views, but not his good intentions?

Such a defense of Roosevelt is hard to maintain in light of the following anecdote related by Burt Folsom. During the period before the official revaluation at $35 an ounce in 1934, the president had the authority to set the gold price at will, and dabbled with it daily, relying on an absurd theory put forward by two Cornell professors that boosting gold prices would raise farm income:

> On November 3...Morgenthau suggested to Roosevelt a 19 to 22 cent rise in price and Roosevelt responded that he wanted 21 cents. Why? "It is a lucky number," Roosevelt said laughing, "because it's three times seven." Morgenthau later wrote in his diary, "If anybody ever knew how we really set the gold price through a combination of lucky numbers, etc., I think they would be frightened."[13]

However well meant the joke, it's hard not to see the cynicism and arbitrariness that often characterized decision-making by the president and his New Deal advisers. Good intentions and emergency need were the excuse for every act of random decision-making, every repudiation of previous law and precedent, every arrogation of power by the Federal government. That too might begin to sound familiar.

The National Recovery Administration: Big Government and Big Business Join Forces

Many grade school discussions of the National Recovery Administration—the epitome of the (first) New Deal approach to battling the Great Depression—talk of businesses drawing up their codes of fair competition as if Roosevelt had merely offered helpful suggestions. In reality, of course, the only way to make the NRA codes "work" was to enforce their provisions on the small producers, once the big producers (and big labor unions) had hammered out the code for a given industry. Countless producers were fined or jailed, such as Jacob Maged, a Jersey City dry cleaner. Burt Folsom describes the fate of Maged, who apparently believed that he lived in a system of free enterprise:

> Maged had been pressing pants for twenty-two years and his low prices and quality work had kept him competitive with larger tailor shops in the better parts of town. The NRA Cleaners and Dyers Code demanded that 40 cents be charged to press a suit. Maged, despite repeated warnings, insisted on charging his customers only 35 cents. "You can't tell me how to run my business," Maged insisted. When threatened with jail, he said, "If you can send me to jail, go ahead."
>
> Not only was Maged thrown in jail, he was also slapped with a hundred-dollar fine. "We think that this is the only way to enforce the NRA," said Abraham Traube, a director of the NRA code authority for the Cleaners and Dyers Board of Trade. "If we did the same thing in New York City we would soon get the whole industry in line."[14]

As Folsom's story illustrates, the notion of a "uniform price" was not a gift to business as New Deal proponents believe. On the contrary, by insisting that all producers in an industry charge a minimum price, the NRA helped *big* business by taking away the main tool with which smaller producers could compete. For example, Carl Pharis ran a tire manufacturing company in Ohio and employed more than 1,000 people. Although his operation was a respectable size, he could not offer the nationwide distribution and support services of Goodyear, Firestone, and Goodrich. The only way Pharis could survive (and indeed thrive) was to—in his words— "make the best possible rubber tire and sell it at the lowest price consistent with a modest but safe profit." Yet the NRA code—formulated by the big companies, certainly not by Pharis Tire and Rubber Company—would render his business model illegal. As Pharis explained:

The Government deliberately raised our prices up towards the prices at which the big companies wanted to sell, at which they could make a profit... where more easily, with much less loss, they could come down and 'get us' and where, bound by N.R.A. decrees, we could not use lower prices, although we could have lowered them and still made a decent profit.[15]

Perhaps the most outrageous injustice occurred in the Schechter case, which was appealed to the Supreme Court and led (in 1935) to the over-turning of the original National Industrial Recovery Act as unconstitutional. The Schechter brothers were chicken butchers in Brooklyn, and were subject to the NRA's Code of Fair Competition for the Live Poultry Industry of the Metropolitan Area in and about the City of New York. Amity Shlaes describes the portions of the code that would prove relevant to the Schechter case:

Section 2 of article 7 declared that it was prohibited "knowingly to purchase or sell for human consumption culls or other produce that is unfit for that purpose."... The code prohibited "straight killing," defined it as "killing on the basis of official grade." The rule meant that customers might select a coop or a half coop of chickens for purchase, but they did not "have the right to make any selection of particular birds."[16]

The Schechters were accused (among other code violations) of selling unfit chickens. However, the evidence against them "in the end, was based on the selection of ten chickens, which was then reduced to three suspect chickens, which, upon autopsy by the health authorities, turned out to include only one unhealthy chicken. It was an 'eggbound' chicken [meaning that] eggs, upon its slaughter, were discovered to have lodged inside it, something that would have been hard for the Schechters to detect before sale."[17] This was the only "crime" that related to anything

Roosevelt's Jack-Booted Thugs

John T. Flynn—a contemporary critic of the New Deal—describes how the Roosevelt administration achieved industry "compliance" with its compassionate plans to help producers:

> "The NRA was discovering it could not enforce its rules. Black markets grew up. Only the most violent police methods could procure enforcement. In Sidney Hillman's garment industry the code authority employed enforcement police. They roamed through the garment district like storm troopers. They could enter a man's factory, send him out, line up his employees, subject them to minute interrogation, take over his books on the instant. Night work was forbidden. Flying squadrons of these private coat-and-suit police went through the district at night, battering down doors with axes looking for men who were committing the crime of sewing together a pair of pants at night."[1]
>
> —Quoted in **Larry Reed**

"Great Myths of the Great Depression" (Mackinac Center for Public Policy, 1998).

that would strike the average person as actually criminal. Nonetheless, the Schechter brothers were found guilty of violating the NRA code, and fined $7,425—the equivalent of more than $100,000 at today's prices. One of the brothers received three months in jail, while his other brothers received lighter sentences.

During testimony when the conviction was appealed to the Supreme Court, the absurdity of the NRA was evident:

[Justice James Clark] McReynolds wanted to probe the meaning of straight killing, and he started with the chickens.

"How many are there in a coop?" There were thirty to forty, according to the size of the coops. "Then when the commission man delivers them to the slaughterhouse, they are in coops?" They were in coops. "And if he undertakes to sell them, he must have straight killing?" He must have straight killing, yes. As [Schechter lawyer Joseph] Heller put it: "His customer is not permitted to select the ones he wants. He must put his hand in the coop when he buys from the slaughterhouse and take the first chicken that comes to hand. He has to take that."

At this point there was laughter in the court.

Then Justice McReynolds asked: "Irrespective of the quality of the chicken?"

Irrespective of the quality of the chicken, Heller replied.

Later on, Justice Sutherland asked, "Well suppose however that all the chickens have gone over to one end of the coop?" (More laughter.)[18]

Although the Supreme Court would overturn the absurdity of the NRA, they were not nearly so bold after FDR's attempt to pack the Court with more justices who would see the wisdom of the New Deal. Rather than risk their (waning) sphere of power against the charismatic Roosevelt in an open confrontation, the Supreme Court became more compliant with the New Deal. Roosevelt, for his part, dropped his plan to pack the Court once it stopped throwing out his legislative victories.

How the New Deal Helped Poor People Go Hungry

Perhaps the most heart-wrenching scene from John Steinbeck's classic novel occurs when starving Americans watch as food is deliberately destroyed:

[A]nd they stand still and watch the potatoes float by, listen to the screaming pigs being killed in a ditch and covered with quicklime, watch the mountains of oranges slop down to a

> putrefying ooze; and in the eyes of the people there is a failure; and in the eyes of the hungry there is a growing wrath. In the souls of the people the grapes of wrath are filling and growing heavy, growing heavy for the vintage.[19]

Steinbeck did not invent these tales to make for good reading. During the 1930s, sellers really did destroy food in order to raise prices. This strikes many people as a horrendous indictment of the profit-based capitalist system.

But the truth is that this absurd outcome could only happen through government coercion. On a free market with competition, it would be foolish for any individual orange seller to douse part of his crop with gasoline. His actions, it is true, would raise orange prices, but the benefits would spill over onto all other orange producers as well, even if they didn't restrict their production. In fact, the higher prices would encourage his rivals to *boost* their production of oranges. And even if all of the domestic orange producers formed a cartel, they would still be unable to prevent foreign producers from sending more oranges to the United States, or to prevent others Americans from entering the industry.

With a free market in agriculture, if farmers were unable to make a living, the most inefficient would stop planting and would turn to some other line of work. This would reduce future harvests, it is true. But it wouldn't be a waste of resources, it would be a redirection of resources into more profitable crops or products. Yet in a free market, even those marginal farmers who needed to switch occupations wouldn't destroy already existing crops—they would instead slash prices to unload the surplus. After all, one doesn't usually see department stores burning unsold Halloween costumes on November 1.

Alas, the United States did not enjoy a free market in agriculture during the Great Depression. Just as Hoover before him, FDR sought to raise farm prices, but simple subsidies led to ever growing inventories. The "logical" next step of deliberate supply restrictions—which occurred under Hoover—was expanded once Roosevelt took power. Jim Powell explains:

> By the time the [Agricultural Adjustment Act] became law and key people were recruited, corn, cotton, tobacco, and wheat were already planted, and livestock operations were moving along. The contemplated output restrictions wouldn't take effect until the following year. So some of the New Dealers began to think their only option, if they wanted to force up farm prices soon, was to destroy crops already planted.... Agriculture Department officials signed up about a million cotton farmers, and they were paid $100 million to plow under some 10 million acres of farmland.... Hog farmers were paid to slaughter some 6 million baby pigs. Economic historian Broadus Mitchell noted that "Most of this pork, under agreement of the government with the packers, became fertilizer; less than a tenth was saved as food and distributed in relief." Mitchell added, "Over 12,000 acres of tobacco were plowed under. California cling peaches were permitted to rot in the orchard."[20]

Harsh New Deal critic John T. Flynn noted the hypocrisy of the government's actions: "[While Agriculture Secretary Henry A.] Wallace was paying out hundreds of millions to kill millions of hogs, burn oats, plow under cotton, the Department of Agriculture issued a bulletin telling the

Books You're Not Supposed to Read

Rethinking the Great Depression, Gene Smiley (Chicago: Ivan R. Dee, 2002)

FDR's Folly: How Roosevelt and His New Deal Prolonged the Great Depression, Jim Powell (New York: Three Rivers Press, 2003)

The Forgotten Man: A New History of the Great Depression, Amity Shlaes (New York: HarperCollins, 2007)

nation that the great problem of our time was our failure to produce enough food."[21]

Old Age Insurance: Not Really Insurance, and Neither Social nor Secure

Not all of the New Deal initiatives became permanent, but of those that did, perhaps the most beloved by the public is Social Security, and in particular its old-age insurance provisions. Workers pay "contributions" taken from each paycheck, and then upon retirement begin "collecting Social Security." In addition, Social Security also provides support for the disabled and the survivors of the death of a breadwinner. The system seems fair and utterly essential, and most Americans are probably puzzled that their country waited until 1935 to implement it.

But upon reflection, the actual format of Social Security is odd. For one thing, the private sector has pension funds and other retirement vehicles, as well as disability and life insurance policies. The legitimate functions of Social Security do not require government provision per se. Even if one wants to argue that the government needs to ensure that *everyone* has a safety net, it still does not follow that the federal government itself needs to administer the program. For an analogy, the government requires that all drivers carry vehicle insurance, but it doesn't collect premiums and pay out claims. On the contrary, the government simply mandates that users of its roads buy adequate policies from private insurers.

This is not a pure armchair thought experiment. Senator Bennett Clark offered an amendment to the Social Security Act that would have allowed employers to opt out of the system so long as they offered their employees pensions with better benefits. Senator Robert M. La Follette, a strong supporter of the original version, objected to offering citizens a choice among plans:

If we shall adopt [the Clark] amendment, the government having determined to set up a federal system of old-age insurance
will provide, in its own bill creating that system, competition
which in the end may destroy the federal system. . . . It would
be inviting and encouraging competition with its own plan
which ultimately would undermine and destroy it.[22]

One obvious reason that the government wanted its monopoly is that
it could then spend the overpayments on other goodies. That is to say,
throughout its history, in each year workers' contributions to Social Security have exceeded the benefits paid to retirees and other beneficiaries.
The difference was then spent by the government, to reduce the amount
it needed to borrow from the private sector to finance its deficit.

To be sure, on the books the Social Security program is kept distinct
from other government activities. There technically exists a "trust fund"
that has accumulated all of the excess payments since the founding of the
system. However, the trust fund does not consist of, say, billions of dollars worth of corporate stock that can be sold off when payroll taxes no
longer cover benefits in a given year. On the contrary, the trust fund is
simply a stockpile of IOUs issued by the federal government itself, put
there when the government spent the excess payroll contributions on current items.

This is a crucial point that is often overlooked in discussions of the
solvency of Social Security. Because the system is in truth a giant Ponzi
scheme—in which the current generation of workers pays retirees, in the
hopes that the *next* generation of workers will be taxed to finance the
retirement of today's workers—it is vulnerable to demographic changes.
As the Baby Boomers reach retirement, the age distribution of American
society tilts more and more towards the elderly. In other words, as time
passes, there are relatively fewer and fewer workers supporting a growing number of people collecting Social Security benefits. Because of this

demographic trend, payroll taxes will have to be increased, benefits will have to be reduced, or both.

But to return to the issue of the trust fund: most analysts, when discussing the need for reform, base their projections on when the deficit between incoming payroll taxes and outgoing benefit payments will have whittled away the trust fund. These analyses thus treat the government debt held by the Social Security Administration in the same way that a private corporation would view its holdings of Treasury bonds as genuine assets.

However, from the general public's point of view, it's not reassuring to know that the Social Security trust fund holds claims on the federal government—meaning the taxpayers. In truth, the crisis in Social Security will arrive *not* when the trust fund is depleted, but when the deficit first appears and the (phony) trust fund stops growing. At that point, the government will have to increase (general) taxes, increase the federal deficit, cut spending, or implement some combination of these measures. According to the most recent CBO projection, this crunch will begin in 2019.[23]

Incidentally, the vulnerability of the Social Security system to demographic changes is *not* a characteristic of old-age provision itself, but is instead entirely due to the Ponzi scheme nature of FDR's program. If workers' "contributions" to Social Security were actually invested as pension fund contributions are, then the benefit payments a retiree received would be tied to what he had invested over his career, *not* to the size of the working population from whom income could be siphoned. Now it is true that in a macro sense, retirees are always "living off of" the work performed by the current generation of laborers. Regardless of where the money comes from, when a retired person buys food at the grocery store, she is in a loose sense skimming off of the output yielded by current farmers.

However, the crucial difference between Social Security and a genuine retirement plan is that through decades of legitimate savings and investment, retirees in a private system have provided more capital equipment for the younger workers who take their place. Their savings enhance the productivity of the next generation of workers, and so there is a greater total crop out of which the retirees get their cut. In contrast, under FDR's scheme, FICA payroll deductions are spent the moment the government receives them. The capital stock does not grow because of the hundreds of billions in forfeited consumption (forfeited through taxes) endured by workers every year; their abstinence is simply used to enlarge the government's consumption.

The looming crisis in Social Security is due to its coercive and fraudulent nature. Demographic changes pose no threat to a market-based retirement system.

The Works Progress Administration: Bad Economics, Good Politics

The New Deal "public works" approach to fighting the Depression was epitomized in the Works Progress Administration (WPA), created by FDR's presidential order and funded through the Emergency Relief Appropriation Act of 1935. Until its termination in 1943, the WPA used billions of federal dollars to give jobs to almost 8 million of the unemployed. Supporters of the WPA thought it was obviously a wonderful agency, which not only provided employment for those shut out by the cruel market, but also created tangible additions to the nation's wealth, such as schools and bridges. Who but a miserly misanthrope could possibly criticize Roosevelt's altruistic program?

Surprising as it may sound to some, the WPA was actually a terrible idea from an economic point of view, and it delayed American recovery from the Depression. To see why, we need to first remind ourselves of why there were so many unemployed people in the first place. The Federal Reserve in the 1920s—especially after it decided to help the Bank of

England in 1927—had flooded credit markets. This lowered interest rates and fueled an investment and speculative boom. Firms started hiring workers and bought resources to begin long-term projects.

After the crash in 1929, prices needed to adjust to channel the available resources and workers to make the best of the situation. Previous bad investments were sunk costs at that point. For an analogy, the American economy in late 1929 was like a construction site where the home builder realizes to his shock that his blueprints have been based on a wildly inflated count of the number of available bricks. When the builder realizes his men won't have enough bricks to finish the house as depicted in his blueprints, the first thing he does is tell everyone to "Stop working!" He needs to halt the further waste of scarce resources until he can figure out how to best reallocate what he has. Once he revises his blueprints, in light of the true brick supply, then everyone can get back to work.

The crucial point, however, is that even if the revised plan eventually calls for all of the workers on the construction site to begin contributing to the redesigned (and more modest) house, they probably won't all be needed the first day after the blueprints are revised. For example, those workers who had been busy painting a deck may be "idle" for weeks, because the revised blueprint no longer has a deck at all, and the painters won't be needed until the rooms of the new house are ready. This is a decent analogy for the situation that many businesses found themselves in during the Great Depression: after the bursting of the unsustainable bubble in 1929, employers had to reassess their needs for workers and resources. Market prices help to make this happen. If producers can't find customers, they probably need to lower their prices. If displaced workers can't find work quickly, they probably need to lower their wage demands. As the economy grows, labor becomes more valuable and wages rise.

The policies of the Hoover and Roosevelt administrations, however, sabotaged this recovery process, and explain why unemployment rates remained shockingly high for an entire decade. The most obvious of course was Hoover's insistence that businesses not cut wages, even as all other prices plummeted. But the WPA hampered recovery as well. (Note that the official figures maintained by the Bureau of Labor Statistics—the ones I used in the previous chapter—included WPA beneficiaries as part of the unemployed work force who could not find jobs in the private sector.) By giving the unemployed an option that paid well enough, the WPA siphoned workers away from truly productive tasks that would have restored the economy to a long-run sustainable condition. To put it bluntly, when we wonder, "Why were so many people unemployed for so long during the New Deal?" part of the answer is, "Because the government paid them to not find a job."

As with Roosevelt's confiscation of gold, the WPA fiasco was not an honest mistake due to faulty economic views. On the contrary, because the WPA placed billions of dollars at the president's discretion, it gave him incredible power to influence elections. After Congress initially allocated $4.8 billion for the WPA in 1935, "state governors had to come hat in hand to Washington hoping to persuade the president to build roads, dams, bridges, and model cities in their states."[24] Roosevelt's reelection team directed the WPA funds to precisely those states that they believed would be up for grabs in the 1936 election:

> With notepad in hand, [Emil] Hurja would tell the Democratic high command, "We have this state for sure—waste no effort on it. We are certain to lose that state. Ignore it." And then, "Now here is a doubtful state that may be lost or won." With Hurja's advice, Postmaster General Farley, who directed the flow of funds for the Democrats, would signal the announcement of new WPA projects and relief programs or designate speakers and campaign materials for those states that Hurja's notebook indicated were doubtful.[25]

The case of Pennsylvania provides the most damning evidence of the nefarious uses to which Democrats put WPA funds. (Of course, Republicans had been just as corrupt during Hoover's term in their disbursement of Reconstruction Finance Corporation bank loans.) In 1932, Hoover had carried Pennsylvania, but Roosevelt's team eyed it as a possible Democratic prize in the 1936 election. In 1936, WPA appropriations increased more than 3,000 percent in the state, the highest in the nation. Analyses of Pennsylvania counties showed a clear correlation between those carried by Roosevelt and those receiving the most federal relief.[26] In fact, one county chairman in Pennsylvania actually sent out the following letter to a constituent:

> Dear Madam:
>
> I am very much surprised that you have not responded to our previous letter requesting your contribution in the amount of $28.08 to Indiana County Democratic Campaign Committee, as I was sure that you appreciated your position to such an extent that you would make this contribution willingly and promptly. I must, however, now advise you that unless your contribution in the above amount is received promptly it will be necessary to place your name on the list of those who will not be given consideration for any other appointment after the termination of the emergency relief work, which as you know will terminate in the near future.[27]

Some government make-work programs were laughable follies. One such representative, of which there were many, was an alleged dream city built by the New Dealer's Resettlement Administration. Located in Nebraska, the project was called Ak-Sar-Ben (Nebraska spelled backwards). This community on the Platte River might have been idyllic, but no one came to live there.[28] The project was, in real terms, a bust. In political terms, of course, it wasn't. It was patronage. And that is the bottom line. The New Deal was, in large part, a matter of government coercion, corruption, force, and fraud. But that's not the usual description you get in the history books.

Chapter 7

THE MYTH OF WARTIME PROSPERITY

Guess What?

- Wars don't make countries richer
- Official statistics showing wartime "prosperity" are misleading
- Markets work better than socialism in making tanks and bombers

Maybe you bought this book already believing that central planning—big government or a socialist style economy—doesn't work during normal times, let alone during a depression. And maybe you already realized that reckless deficit spending doesn't make a country richer. As commonsensical as these two points seem, they're still pretty much ignored in Washington. But even people who understand them fall prey to another myth: that somehow widespread death and destruction promote economic growth, and that World War II got us out of the Great Depression. But it's not true.

When a nation diverts millions of its most productive workers, as well as large quantities of steel, rubber, gasoline, and other scarce resources, away from the production of cars, radios, and other consumer goods, and into the production of tanks, bombers, and munitions that will be shipped overseas and destroyed...well, that makes the people on the home front poorer. And what is true for the United States is true also for Europe and Japan, which on top of siphoned resources also had their factories blown to smithereens. Any child would understand that World War II was devastating not just in human terms, but also for the global economy.

Yet most Americans have been taught the myth of "wartime prosperity." Ironically, even many foes of FDR subscribe to this explanation: "It

145

Not the Best Way to Boost Your Economy

"War prosperity is like the prosperity that an earthquake or a plague brings."

—Ludwig von Mises

Nation, State, and Economy (New York: New York University Press, [1919] 1983).

wasn't the New Deal that got us out of the Depression, it was the war!" These two alternative theories, however, rest on the same faulty premise that massive government spending can "create jobs" and "stimulate aggregate demand." If the conservative recognizes that Roosevelt's spending on canals and drafting men into the WPA was no way to fix the economy, then he should also understand that Roosevelt's spending on tanks and drafting men into the Army was no solution, either.

Before proceeding, I should clarify one thing: I am *not* claiming in this chapter that Franklin Roosevelt was wrong to lead the United States into war against the Axis powers. Instead, I'm refuting the common assumption that our entry into the war provided direct *economic* benefits. On the contrary, the war was incredibly costly, and represented an enormous drain on American resources.

Now sometimes expensive things are worth buying. Many scientists believe that government funding of space exploration and particle accelerators is well worth the cost. By the same token, many doctors believe that government funding of cancer research also represents a wise use of tax dollars. But the point is, we shouldn't fool ourselves into thinking that these programs are free. It takes real, tangible resources—including commodities such as rubber and oil, but also more advanced resources such as computer time and the man-hours of trained scientists—to place telescopes into orbit and to run medical laboratories. There are other goods and services that those scarce resources could have produced, but which humans will now never enjoy because they were instead devoted to government projects. Economic science cannot by itself say whether one pattern of resource usage is better than the other, but we must realize that the tradeoff exists.

From a strictly pragmatic perspective, it makes sense to do something if its benefits outweigh the costs. There were many non-pecuniary reasons for waging war against Nazi Germany and Imperial Japan, and they may very well have justified the immense costs of our entry into the conflict. But we must not confuse our costs with our benefits. Whatever virtues the reader attributes to World War II, "pulling us out of the Depression" was not one of them.

The Immortal Error: The Broken Window Fallacy

At the heart of the myth of wartime prosperity is "the broken window fallacy," which was definitively debunked by the great classical liberal economist Frédéric Bastiat in the nineteenth century. In this tale, some hooligan children throw a brick through a shopkeeper's window. A crowd gathers and reflects on the scene, while the shopkeeper of course is furious. Yet soon enough someone in the crowd remarks that the apparent curse is actually a blessing, because the shopkeeper will now be forced to buy a new window, which will provide employment for the glazier. The glazier, in turn, will have a higher income, and so will spend more money on the merchants whom he patronizes. Thus the miscreants paradoxically provided ripples of economic prosperity when they destroyed the shopkeeper's property.

Of course, this analysis can't be right. If it were, then communities could grow fantastically wealthy by handing adolescent boys buckets of golf balls and turning them loose on the town. The flaw, Bastiat points out, is focusing on the extra business for the glazier, while ignoring the extra expense for the shopkeeper. The gain in business for the glazier is offset by the loss in business for, say, the tailor whom the shopkeeper might have hired to make him a new suit had he not had to buy a new

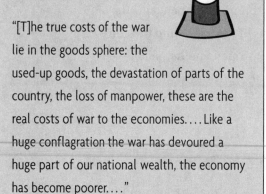

Destruction Isn't Constructive

"[T]he true costs of the war lie in the goods sphere: the used-up goods, the devastation of parts of the country, the loss of manpower, these are the real costs of war to the economies.... Like a huge conflagration the war has devoured a huge part of our national wealth, the economy has become poorer...."

—Joseph Schumpeter

"The Crisis of the Tax State," in idem, *The Economics and Sociology of Capitalism*, Richard Swedberg, ed. (Princeton, N.J.: Princeton University Press, 1991), 118–19.

window. And one person is definitely poorer—the shopkeeper, who has to both replace the broken window and forfeit a new suit. As Bastiat shows, economics is really common sense: when a hooligan destroys the window of someone in the community, then that person is (and the community is) one window poorer.

A Billion Wrongs Don't Make a Right

At the simplest level, the myth of wartime prosperity is the broken window fallacy writ large. The renowned economic journalist Henry Hazlitt explains:

Though some [learned statisticians and professors of economics in our best universities] would disdain to say that there are net benefits in small acts of destruction, they see almost endless benefits in enormous acts of destruction. They tell us how much better off economically we all are in war than in peace. They see "miracles of production" which it requires a war to achieve. And they see a world made prosperous by an enormous "accumulated" or "backed-up" demand. In Europe, after World War II, they joyously counted the houses, the whole cities that had been leveled to the ground and that "had to be replaced." In America they counted the houses that could not be built during the war, the nylon stockings that could not be

148

supplied, the worn-out automobiles and tires, the obsolescent radios and refrigerators.[1]

Hazlitt does not leave his readers in suspense, and quickly explains the error in such thinking:

> It was merely our old friend, the broken-window fallacy, in new clothing, and grown fat beyond recognition. This time it was supported by a whole bundle of related fallacies. It confused *need* with *demand*. The more war destroys, the more it impoverishes, the greater is the postwar need. Indubitably. But need is not demand.... The needs of India today are incomparably greater than the needs of America. But its purchasing power, and therefore the "new business" that it can stimulate, are incomparably smaller.[2]

It is not destruction—or what destruction brings, poverty—that stimulates economies, it is productivity. The postwar economies of Japan and Germany—

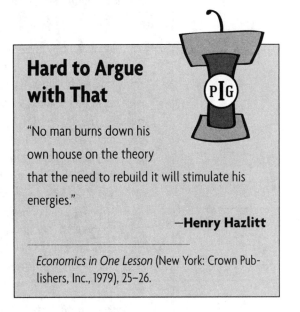

Hard to Argue with That

"No man burns down his own house on the theory that the need to rebuild it will stimulate his energies."

—Henry Hazlitt

Economics in One Lesson (New York: Crown Publishers, Inc., 1979), 25–26.

despite the tremendous bombings they endured—outperformed the economies of India and Nigeria because of the superior training, tools, and institutional structures they enjoyed. As Hazlitt stressed, a nation can't grow rich simply by "needing" more products—its workers have to have the ability to produce them in order for these same people, in their roles as consumers, to have the income to purchase the products.

As with the tale of the broken window, here too the Allied bombings did indeed make the Germans and Japanese poorer. The labor power and

Were Allied Bombers the Mother of Innovation?

A more sophisticated argument for the (alleged) benefits of destruction is that the German and Japanese economies benefited from having state-of-the-art factories and equipment competing with the older models still in use in the United States. Once again we turn to Hazlitt to spot the fallacy:

> [I]f this were really a clear net advantage, Americans could easily offset it by immediately wrecking their old plants, junking all the old equipment. In fact, all manufacturers in all countries could scrap all their old plants and equipment every year and erect new plants and install new equipment.
>
> The simple truth is that there is an optimum rate of replacement, a best time for replacement. It would be an advantage for a manufacturer to have his factory and equipment destroyed by bombs only if the time had arrived when, through deterioration and obsolescence, his plant and equipment had already acquired a null or negative value and the bombs fell just when he should have called in a wrecking crew or ordered new equipment anyway.
>
> **—Henry Hazlitt**

Economics in One Lesson, 29.

other resources that went into housing and factory construction after the war could instead have been devoted to the production of new pieces of wealth. But as with the shopkeeper who had to abandon his hopes for a new suit in order to restore his shop to its previous condition, so too the people of Germany and Japan had to slog away for years merely to restore their countries' wealth to prewar levels. Even though many foolish economists viewed this as a blessing, in fact it was a curse to have decades of hard work destroyed in seconds by enemy bombers.

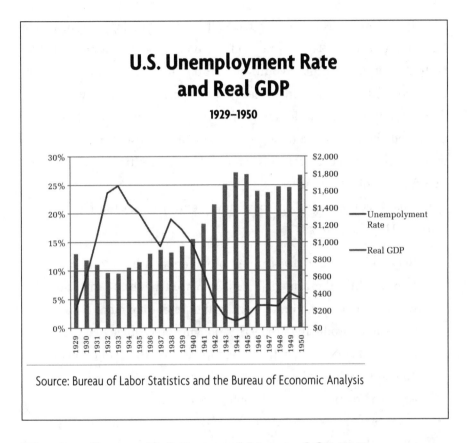

U.S. Unemployment Rate and Real GDP

1929–1950

Source: Bureau of Labor Statistics and the Bureau of Economic Analysis

Wartime Prosperity? Damned Lies and Statistics

Even if it's common sense that killing workers and blowing up factories can't possibly be helpful to an economy, we do have to acknowledge
the apparent statistical evidence showing that World War II really *did*
seem to pull the United States out of the Great Depression. In particular,
as the chart above shows, the official measures of unemployment and real
Gross Domestic Product finally turned around as the United States geared
up for war.

In a series of books and papers spanning more than a decade, economist Robert Higgs has dismantled the seemingly impressive evidence
for wartime prosperity.[3] Most obvious, how can we say that the war
"cured" the unemployment problem, when it achieved this goal merely

by shipping millions of men overseas? To give an analogy, suppose that FDR announced in 1940 that in an effort to fight the depression, all able-bodied unemployed men would be shipped to African jungles (where they would face lions and disease). That policy would have brought down the official unemployment rate, yet it obviously would not have promoted actual economic recovery. Had FDR suggested something this monstrous as a "cure" for mass unemployment, citizens would have rightfully recoiled in horror.

Flippant as the jungle analogy may seem, it is not too far from the truth, as Higgs explains:

> Between 1940 and 1944, unemployment fell by...7.45 million...while the armed forces increased by 10.87 million. Even if one views eliminating civilian unemployment as tantamount to producing prosperity, one must recognize that placing...146 persons...in the armed forces to gain a reduction of 100 persons in civilian unemployment was a grotesque way to achieve prosperity, even if a job were a job.
>
> In fact, however, military "jobs" differed categorically. Often, they entailed substantial risks of death, dismemberment, and other physical and psychological injuries. Military service yielded little pay under harsh conditions and, like it or not, lasted for the duration of the war. Sustained exposure to combat drove many men insane...Physical casualties included 405,399 dead and 670,846 wounded.... To treat military jobs as commensurate with civilian jobs during World War II, as economists do in computing the tradeoffs between them, betrays a monumental obtuseness to their realities.[4]

Higgs goes on to point out that similar conceptual problems plague the official measures of output during the war years. To understand Higgs's critique, we must first review the standard procedure for measuring Gross

National Product (GNP), or, as the economists now prefer, Gross Domestic Product (GDP). Gross Domestic Product calculates the country's total economic production not by making a huge laundry list of all of the cars, computers, haircuts, and Happy Meals produced, but by adding up all their prices, multiplied by the number of units sold of each product. When calculating GDP, economists therefore count up the total spending on American products by consumers, businesses, foreigners, and the government.

Already we see a major problem in relying on official GDP statistics as a gauge of overall economic production. When the government massively expands its own spending—as happened from 1940 to 1945—it boosts the official GDP, because government spending is one component of this official measure. The problem though is that an extra million dollars in goods and services as determined by a Pentagon contract is not as productive as when consumers spend one million dollars on goods and services produced in the private sector.

Books You're Not Supposed to Read

Economics in One Lesson, Henry Hazlitt (New York: Crown Publishers, Inc., 1979)

Depression, War, and Cold War, Robert Higgs (New York: Oxford University Press, 2006)

Against Leviathan, Robert Higgs (Oakland, C.A.: The Independent Institute, 2004)

The Costs of War: America's Pyrrhic Victories, John V. Denson ed. (New Brunswick, N.J.: Transaction Publishers, 1999, second edition)

Why? Because government officials have fewer incentives to find the best quality hardware at the best price. In fact, the opposite is the case, especially in wartime when the sense of urgency means that money is more likely to be spent *now* with little regard for price. But even in peacetime, the familiar "use it or lose it" mentality reigning in D.C. ensures that price is not what guides expenditure; procurement officers who come in under budget are likely to see their budgets slashed since they obviously didn't "need" the money. And since all government departments want

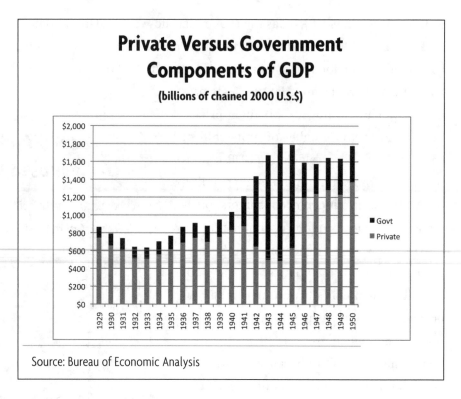

Source: Bureau of Economic Analysis

more money, their incentive is to spend more money. This difference in incentives explains why one billion dollars spent on a pork barrel project—such as an overpriced, nearly vacant government office building—is not at all comparable to one billion dollars spent by private investors looking for a profit.

Because government spending is not nearly as good an indicator of true economic value as private spending, we should be suspicious of boosts in official GDP numbers when they are caused by bursts in government spending. Yet this is exactly what happened during World War II, as the chart above shows.

Yet the problem gets worse, as Higgs pushes the critique even further. The U.S. government did not rely solely on taxes and borrowing to raise the funds it spent on the war effort. Quite the contrary, the government—freed from the constraints of the gold standard—embarked on a massive inflationary spree. So we now have the additional wrinkle, that much of the GDP could be attributed to the printing press inflating the numbers.

Now in fairness to the economic statisticians, we should clarify that they are not completely naïve: the standard criterion for economic growth looks at "real GDP," meaning the total dollar amount produced in a given year, *after adjusting for price hikes*. To give a simple example: If the government doubled the money supply in a year, causing prices on average to double, then the same physical output of goods and services would correspond to a doubling in the (nominal) GDP figure. But the statisticians would correct for this distortion by using a "deflator" based on the increase in the prices of milk, eggs, and other items typically purchased by households. So in normal circumstances, a government can't "cheat" and boost its official GDP numbers just by running the printing press, because the statisticians would take into account the rising price inflation. Doubling the money supply would basically double all prices, leaving "real GDP" unchanged.

Here is where the interpretation of the apparent wartime "prosperity" gets a little more complex. During the war the government imposed price controls, forcibly *preventing* the Consumer Price Index from rising as quickly as it otherwise would have done. But this means that the historical prices we have recorded for these years are meaningless, rendering it impossible for economic historians to adjust the data on historical dollar expenditures to account for the (suppressed) inflation. So the carefully constructed measures of "inflation-adjusted gross domestic output" during the 1940s are about as meaningful as the economic statistics reported by the Soviet Union. These wartime economic statistics, as Higgs concludes, are "essentially arbitrary."[5] The government effectively made it illegal for market prices to signal how much inflation the Fed was pumping into the system, and so it is very misleading to compute GDP during the war years with the traditional techniques.

Another thing the official statistics do not show us is how many sacrifices civilians made during the war. Not only did they sacrifice goods for wartime production, but if they weren't drafted they often had to relocate to go where the jobs were—in factories focused on war production. Rent controls imposed at the time kept prices artificially low, but at the cost of keeping apartments in an increasingly shabby state of disrepair. Housing shortages were famous—especially in cities like Washington (you can get a glimpse of this in the classic 1943 comedy *The More the Merrier*)—or where war production factories were located. Some consumer goods simply weren't made at all. Automobile makers didn't build cars during the war, they built military vehicles. Gasoline, shoes, coffee, and many other items were rationed, and self-sacrifice was, of course, promoted by the government as a patriotic duty—and perhaps it was, but that doesn't mean that the war brought "prosperity."

Central Planning: Bad in Peacetime, Deadly in War

As we have seen, it is a myth that the gargantuan deficits of the war years finally pulled the United States out of the Depression. To repeat an earlier point, those who oppose the New Deal *can't* simultaneously believe in the fable of wartime prosperity, because the logic is the same: Conservatives who credit military spending with economic recovery are unwittingly endorsing the very same Keynesian pump-priming that they oppose in the realm of domestic spending. Such conservatives are implicitly agreeing with Paul Krugman and others who say that the New Deal failed because it was too timid; according to this view, if FDR had only had the courage to run deficits exceeding 20 percent of GDP when he first came into office—rather than waiting until 1942 to begin this bold policy of borrow-and-spend—then the Depression would have ended by 1937.[6] Indeed, the myth of wartime prosperity leads to the monstrous conclusion that, whatever other things he may have had going against him, at least Adolf Hitler forced Americans to fix their economy.

Fortunately, the reader who generally favors the free market does not need to concede such monstrosities. American participation in the war was perhaps a regrettable necessity, but by no means did the war help the American economy. Wartime production is either destroyed or, in peace, loses most if not all of its value. That is not the way to increase prosperity.

Yet there is a related myth that we should also briefly address. Just as opponents of Keynesian pump-priming in peacetime often endorse the myth of wartime prosperity, so too we often find that conservative proponents of the free market in peacetime suddenly become apostles of central planning during a major war. Even among people who generally acknowledge the superior ability of decentralized entrepreneurs, guided by market prices, to make the crucial decisions of which goods and services will be produced, for some reason all of this faith in capitalism collapses in the face of a foreign military threat.

The following excerpt from a historical account of the war is typical. Note how seamlessly the writer includes economic controls with strictly military operations:

> In 1939, the United States had about 174,000 men in the Army; 126,400 in the Navy; 26,000 in the Army Air Corps; 19,700 in the Marine Corps; and 10,000 in the Coast Guard. At the height of its strength in 1945, the United States had six million in the Army; 3,400,000 in the Navy; 2,400,000 in the Army air forces; 484,000 in the Marine Corps; and 170,000 in the Coast Guard. In 1939, the United States had about 2,500 airplanes and 760 warships. By 1945, it had about 80,000 airplanes and 2,500 warships. The United States used draft laws to build their

armed forces. The United States Selective Service Act became law on September 16, 1940.

Factories in the United States converted from civilian to war production with amazing speed. Firms that had made vacuum cleaners before the war began to produce machine guns. As men went into the armed forces, women took their places in war plants. By 1943, more than two million women were working in American war industries. In shipyards and aircraft plants, Rosie the riveter became a common sight. Officials discovered that women could perform the duties of eight of every 10 jobs normally done by men. [sic!]

Urgent requirements for war matériel caused many shortages in consumer goods. Most governments, both Allied and Axis, had to ration the amount of consumer goods each person could use. In the United States, rationed items included meats, butter, sugar, fats, oil, coffee, canned foods, shoes, and gasoline. Congress gave the president power to freeze prices, salaries, and wages at their levels of September 15, 1942. The United States imposed a special excise tax on such luxury items as jewelry and cosmetics.[7]

Contrary to the quotation above, the market economy is perfectly capable of handling a quick transition from producing one mix of goods to another. In fact, the primary *virtue* of a market economy is that its decentralized structure allows the "man on the spot" to make quick decisions based on localized knowledge. In contrast, a bureaucratic, centrally planned economy requires the managers of shops and factories to communicate their concerns up the chain of command, wait for the officials in charge to revise The Plan, and then send down new orders.

It is a simple fact of engineering that the enormous production of tanks, airplanes, and other wartime goods in the 1940s necessitated a sharp curtailment in civilian consumption. Even so, the government did not need to impose direct rationing and other controls on the home front. Instead, the government could have simply raised taxes and issued new bonds in order to purchase its desired products from military contractors and other firms. The higher taxes and higher interest rates (resulting from the government deficits) would have forced the American public to sharply curtail its spending on consumption, and the lucrative military contracts would have given war-related firms the ability to outbid civilian-related firms in the markets for raw materials and other goods. Individual businesses, seeking only to maximize profit, would have been led as by an Invisible Hand to retool away from civilian production and cater instead to the overall war effort.

Now it is true, even free market economists would argue about how far the boundaries of laissez-faire could be pushed when a capitalist country enters a major war. For example, some economists would argue that conscription was unnecessary, and that the government should have offered compensation packages attractive enough to entice the required number of men to enlist. An all-volunteer force has many advantages, including higher morale, quicker training, and less threat of desertion. (In present times, the fighting prowess of the U.S. military is certainly not handicapped by its lack of coercion in gaining new recruits.) On the other hand, some economists—even those who

Winning by any Means Necessary

"Capitalism is essentially a scheme for peaceful nations. But this does not mean that a nation which is forced to repel foreign aggressors must substitute government control for private enterprise. If it were to do this, it would deprive itself of the most efficient means of defense. There is no record of a socialist nation which defeated a capitalist nation. In spite of their much glorified war socialism, the Germans were defeated in both World Wars."

—Ludwig von Mises

Human Action, Scholar's Edition (Auburn, AL: Ludwig von Mises Institute).

Capitalism Better at Both Butter and Guns

"Not government decrees and the paper work of hosts of people on the government's payroll, but the efforts of private enterprise produced those goods which enabled the American armed forces to win the war and to provide all the material equipment its allies needed for their cooperation.... [T]he interventionists would have us believe that a decree prohibiting the employment of steel for the construction of apartment houses automatically produces airplanes and battleships."

—**Ludwig von Mises**, *Human Action*.

generally oppose government wartime controls—might not push the case quite this far, because they believe that the war required so many men that the government could not possibly have offered enough money to achieve the required number of volunteers.

But putting aside the issue of conscription, the case for wartime controls is weak indeed. Through its extensive price controls, rationing schemes, and high taxes on "excess profits," the U.S. government approached outright central planning of the economy during the war years. All of the standard arguments against socialism apply in this context. Just as entrepreneurs outperform government planners in the inexpensive production of quality goods in peacetime, so they could have done the same in wartime. But price controls and the overwhelming desire to wipe out "war profits" crippled the private sector from discovering better ways of feeding civilians and equipping the military. Prices would have told producers what items were scarce, what items were in surplus, and how to maximize production in order to meet demand—whether it was for tomatoes or bazookas. Precisely because World War II was an unprecedented event, there were no "experts" on transforming civilian production to military production on this scale. When it comes to motivating millions of people to brainstorm and quickly come up with better ways to make a mousetrap (or tank), nothing beats the profit-driven market economy.

Wartime rationing schemes were particularly absurd, because they imposed enormous sacrifices on consumers for no purpose. The most efficient way to make sure necessary resources get to the military in wartime is for the government to use its tax and bond receipts to enter the market and buy what it needs. But crucially, the government needs to let its demand for certain products push up their prices. High prices, on goods needed by the military, would signal their true scarcity, and consumers would adjust their buying accordingly. The important thing is that civilians themselves would decide how to cut their consumption. The government wasn't doing anybody favors by holding down the official prices of necessities, when at the same time it insisted that consumers needed ration cards (in addition to dollar bills) to make their purchases. All the rationing ensured was that, in addition to the overall privation required by the war effort, civilians *also* had to endure a layer of pointless bureaucracy.

In peacetime, the superiority of the market economy over central planning is manifest. When it came to war, the U.S. government stifled its greatest advantage by resorting to the philosophy of its enemies, current (Nazi Germany) and future (Soviet Russia).

Postscript: Ways in which World War II Did Boost American Production

In the interest of balance, we should close this chapter by conceding a few ways in which the outbreak of war *did* legitimately stimulate the U.S. economy. To be sure, for the reasons outlined above, overall the war was incredibly expensive and made Americans poorer. But even so, there were a few ways in which the war boosted the economy.

First, there is the obvious fact that the threat of worldwide tyranny motivated Americans to work much harder and to postpone much more consumption, than they otherwise would have done. De facto, the war emergency spawned a nationwide revival of the Protestant work ethic. In this (limited) respect, some of the increases in official measurements of national production were quite real. Of course, even here it can't be said that the war was *good* for the American people, since there is nothing desirable about additional work per se. (You don't really help a man by egging his house and "motivating" him to get off the couch to clean up the mess, nor do you really improve his condition by threatening to kill his dog unless he saves more.) But in terms of the narrow criterion of total production of material goods and services, the outbreak of the war really did stimulate Americans to produce more.

A second way that World War II really did boost the American economy was the huge increase in foreign demand for U.S. exports. Much to the chagrin of the Germans, American industry—"the arsenal of democracy"—sent enormous quantities of war matériel and other supplies to the Allies, even before Pearl Harbor. From the passage of the Lend-Lease bill in March 1941 through the end of the war, the United States sent some $50 billion worth of goods overseas (in 1940s dollars).[8] Now if U.S. exporters had directly sold these goods to Allied governments in exchange for gold, or even IOUs that were eventually honored, the bolstered demand for U.S. products would have made America richer. The country as a whole would have economically benefited from the war just as surely as the shareholders of Boeing are enriched when a war breaks out and they receive lucrative new contracts. In practice, however, much of the "lent" material was never paid for by the other Allied powers, and instead was picked up by—you guessed it—the U.S. taxpayer.[9]

FDR Finally Gets Big Business on Board

PIG

"If you are going to try to go to war, or to prepare for war, in a capitalist country, you have got to let business make money out of the process or business won't work..."

—**Henry L. Stimson**, U.S. Secretary of War, 1940

Quoted in Robert Higgs, *Depression, War, and Cold War* (New York: Oxford University Press, 2006), 30.

A third way that the war benefited the U.S. economy was the relative advantage it gave to American exporters, since their competitors were either killed or had their factories blown apart. If food poisoning kills 90 percent of the attendees at a conference of accountants, the survivors will probably benefit financially because they will enjoy so much more business than before the tragedy. However, what American exporters gained in this respect was also counterbalanced by the loss to American consumers who could no longer import goods from European companies that were now defunct.

Finally, we come to a fourth way that World War II truly did help "get us out of the Depression." Before the war, businessmen and investors worried about how New Deal policies would punish them and their property rights. The war changed all that. The need to ramp up domestic military preparedness led FDR to replace some of his more starry-eyed New Dealers with practical businessmen. The result, as Robert Higgs points out, was to create a more pro-business atmosphere that actually did help us get out of the Great Depression:

Uncle Sam Wants You! (Unless You're a Socialist)

"Virtually none of [the leftist New Dealers] moved into important positions in the war bureaucracies; many of them lost their positions in the civilian agencies in which they had been serving. By the end of 1943, the liberal diaspora was nearly complete. Almost no real 'New Dealers' remained."

—Historian **Alan Brinkley**,

Quoted in Higgs, 19.

After the outbreak of war in Europe in 1939, if not before, President Roosevelt focused his time and energy on foreign and military affairs. Effective U.S. rearmament...required the cooperation of business people, especially those in control of the nation's biggest corporations....

To accommodate the business titans, FDR enlisted their leadership in a succession of mobilization committees, boards, and agencies.... In June 1940, Roosevelt put a firm foundation under his coalition with big business by naming [Henry L.] Stimson as Secretary of War and publisher Frank Knox, who had been the Republican candidate for vice-president in 1936, as Secretary of the Navy.... Under such leadership, the armed services, which quickly became the greatest buyers in industrial history, were not likely to manage their procurements in a fashion hostile to business.... By the middle of 1942, more than 10,000 business executives had taken positions in federal war agencies.[10]

As we have seen, FDR had no problem demonizing and alienating big business in his fight against the Depression. But when it came to fighting Hitler, he wisely realized that fireside chats and ivory tower plans weren't going to cut it. Many of the extreme New Dealers had to leave the administration, not only to reassure big business, but also because "only business managers had the practical knowledge required to run the war economy—politicians, lawyers, and economists have rather severe limitations when it comes to organizing the production of battleships, bombers, and tanks."[11]

So there were a few ways the war helped America's economy, but I stress that these were *swamped* by the ways in which World War II was a huge burden. World War II was, obviously, incredibly costly in terms of forfeited lives and economic destruction. The apparent end of the Great Depression in the early 1940s is largely a statistical illusion. True prosperity did not return until demobilization, when the federal government relinquished its stranglehold on the American economy and once again allowed private investors and entrepreneurs to direct resources. Inasmuch as President Roosevelt was dead at this point, we can put to rest the claim that "FDR got us out of the Depression."

Chapter 8

THE GREAT DEPRESSION: LESSONS FOR TODAY

he news media has often compared the financial crisis that began in 2007 to the Great Depression, which left the media free to lay the blame on George "Herbert Hoover" Bush and his do-nothing laissez-faire ideology. The election of Barack Obama only intensified the comparison, because he was cast as the modern FDR who could swoop in and rescue capitalism from itself once again. As surprising as it might seem, the talking heads, to a certain degree, have it right: in many respects, Americans *are* reliving the Great Depression. Then as now, the Federal Reserve fueled an unsustainable boom. Then as now, a Republican president responded to the downturn with unprecedented expansions in government spending and meddling with the private sector. And—assuming President Obama fulfills even half of his campaign promises—then as now, the Big Government Republican will be chased out of office by a charismatic Bigger Government Democrat, whose horrible policies will ensure that the economic slump lasts a decade.

The Fed Caused the Housing Boom—and Bust

The housing (and stock market) boom and bust of the 2000s presents an almost textbook illustration of the business cycle theory as outlined

Guess What?

- The Fed caused the boom-bust in housing

- George Bush was like Herbert Hoover—a big government "conservative"

- Barack Obama does sound like FDR— meaning we can expect a long depression

by economists Ludwig von Mises and Friedrich Hayek (who won the Nobel Prize for Economics in 1974). Their theory, the so-called "Austrian business cycle theory," says, in a nutshell, that business cycles of boom and bust are not inherent in a free market economy, but come from outside it—namely, from the actions of government through its monopoly central bank. In a truly free market economy, interest rates would be determined by the supply of savings and the demand for loans. But modern central banks, like the Federal Reserve, are always anxious to reduce interest rates below their free market levels. They do so by flooding the financial sector with new credit, which pushes down interest rates.

The motivation for this chicanery, of course, is that it provides a temporary euphoria, a period of apparent prosperity. At the artificially reduced rates, businesses undertake projects that would have been unprofitable at the higher, true interest rates set by the free market. In effect, what happens is that the Fed creates new money and hands it over to the banks, and they in turn lend it out to enterprising firms. These firms then use the new money to hire workers and bid resources away from others, so they can start their new projects. Business seems good, wages and commodity prices begin rising, and the unemployment rate drops. In short, the injection of artificial credit fuels an economic boom.

The problem, as Mises wrote in 1928, is that "every boom must one day come to an end." Like other prices, the (undistorted) market rate of interest really *means* something. The market rate of interest has the important job of matching up the amount of borrowing with the amount of capital actually being saved. But because of the distortion of credit by the Federal Reserve, businesses begin buying resources and making long-term investments *as if consumers have saved more than they really have*. In fact, the artificially low interest rates actually lead consumers to save less (and spend more) than they normally would.

Mises and Hayek demonstrated that this situation is unsustainable. In a normal market economy, production grows over time because of a growing accumulation of capital equipment, made possible by acts of abstinence (savings). But in a Fed-induced boom, the central bank tries to rush the process; it wants businesses to produce more drill presses *without* consumers having to even temporarily restrict their purchases of radios and fancy dinners.

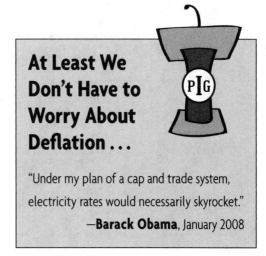

At Least We Don't Have to Worry About Deflation . . .

"Under my plan of a cap and trade system, electricity rates would necessarily skyrocket."
—**Barack Obama**, January 2008

The illusion can last for some years, but it can't last forever. As the boom persists year after year, the structure of production becomes more and more distorted and unsustainable. This is exactly what happened in the United States (and the world) during the housing boom years. When the crisis hits—when it is finally realized that there are insufficient savings to support all the capital ventures that easy money has encouraged—businesses have to retrench, abandon some of their projects, and lay off workers. As painful as this day of reckoning is, the sooner the boom ends and the "slump" begins, the easier the readjustment period will be. True "recovery" starts the moment after the crash.

The Mises-Hayek theory fits the facts of the housing bubble very well. Following the dot-com crash and September 11 attacks, the U.S. economy entered a recession. In order to provide a "soft landing," Federal Reserve chairman Alan Greenspan took the federal funds rate down to 1 percent—the lowest it had been since the 1950s—and held it there for a full year (June 2003 to June 2004). After adjusting for price inflation, the real interest rate during this period was actually *negative*. In June 2004, Greenspan began ratcheting the rate back up, anxious to contain inflation.

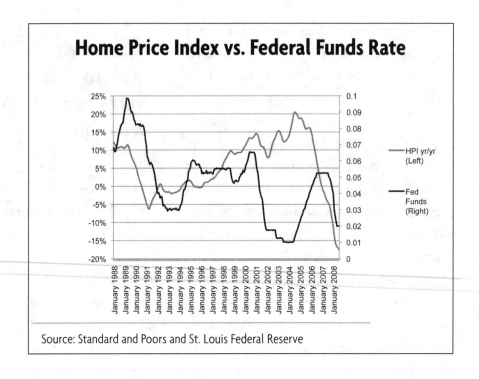

Home Price Index vs. Federal Funds Rate

Source: Standard and Poors and St. Louis Federal Reserve

It is surprising that some analysts still refuse to admit that the Fed's stepping on the gas and then the brake had anything to do with the boom-bust in housing. Basic economic theory says that home prices rise when interest rates (specifically, mortgage rates) fall. The chart above plots the year-over-year percentage increases in the popular S&P/Case-Shiller Home Price Index, versus the federal funds rate.

As the chart illustrates, Greenspan's incredibly easy money policy certainly appears to have fueled the housing boom. As interest rates plummeted, house prices experienced their largest yearly gains. Housing appreciation peaked soon after Greenspan began raising interest rates, with continued rate hikes going hand-in-hand with the slowing and finally popping bubble. (Where the gray line crosses the 0 percent line on the left axis, home prices began falling.)

Many conservatives have pointed to government interventions such as the Community Reinvestment Act (CRA), which pressured banks to approve mortgages for unqualified borrowers, as well as to the privileged positions (through implicit guarantees of their debt) given to Fannie Mae and Freddie Mac, so-called "government sponsored enterprises" that had mission statements calling for increased homeownership among poorer Americans. Time and again, these politically correct organizations were shielded from reform by liberal Democrats like Senator Christopher Dodd of Connecticut and Congressman Barney Frank of Massachusetts.

Now, it is certainly true that these government programs and entities distorted the performance of the market, and channeled too many resources into housing. However, by themselves such programs could not generate a massive boom—not just in real estate but also in the stock market—in which resources were pumped into new housing at the same time that consumers spent more on iPods, clothes, SUVs, and gasoline. For this type of systematic error, in which long-term investment projects were started, even though savings had fallen, a massive distortion in credit markets (through artificially low interest rates) was needed. For that, we need to blame the Fed.

The Myth of Laissez-Faire George Bush

But of course the liberal media did not blame the Fed, it blamed the unregulated greed of capitalism. Even Alan Greenspan, anxious to save his own skin and take the scrutiny off of his interest rate decisions, capitulated and agreed that he had put too much faith in self-regulating financial markets. The liberal argument is that government regulators could have saved us from the financial meltdown that started in the housing bust. But the facts don't support that argument. For one thing, why would government regulators have been better at spotting an unsustainable bubble than the investors whose own money was at risk? For example, as late as December 2005, two Federal Reserve staff economists released a paper arguing that there was no bubble in housing prices.[1] Two who were warning of the housing bubble, on the other hand, were advocates of the Mises-Hayek business cycle theory: fund manager Peter Schiff and Republican Congressman Ron Paul of Texas. To put it starkly, it is hard to believe that Washington bureaucrats can predict future moves of the market better than Wall Street professionals or care more about a hedge fund's returns than the owners themselves. Everything we know about Washington argues against that. Indeed, even when the Bush administration tried to rein in the excesses of Fannie Mae and Freddie Mac before the housing bubble burst, it was the advocates of regulation—Barney Frank and Christopher Dodd and company—who refused to allow any reform of one of their favored constituencies.

A Book You're Not Supposed to Read

Meltdown: A Free Market Look at Why the Stock Market Collapsed, the Economy Tanked, and Government Bailouts Will Make Things Worse, Thomas E. Woods Jr. (Regnery, 2009).

Let me be clear: I am *not* saying that "the market" is always right, while government regulators are always wrong. Clearly, many investors and financial professionals—including especially the ratings agencies—made very serious mistakes during the boom years. The last people who would say "Wall Street can't be wrong" are those who endorse the Hayekian business cycle theory, because it was precisely these analysts who had been warning for years about the dangers of the stock market and the housing bubbles. But however wrong the Wall Street experts were, it is nonsensical to simply assume that government regulators would have done a better job. Anybody can "call" an asset bubble after the fact. A new Federal Office of Backseat Driving would do nothing productive for our economy but would inhibit innovation. Sometimes regulators would miss genuine bubbles (as they did with housing) while other times they mistakenly would "pop" legitimate, sustainable increases in certain prices.

The free market, by its very nature, is self-regulating. It is government interventions that inevitably distort it, often with unintended consequences. The greatest argument that liberal critics have against market-based economics is that the financial meltdown happened under the watch of President George W. Bush. But notwithstanding his rhetoric, George W. Bush was the furthest thing from a free market, small government crusader. He was, by his own description, a "compassionate conservative," or, in other words, a big government man who massively expanded the federal government in ways that no true conservative could ever countenance.

The ballooning of the federal government under George W. Bush's tenure wasn't simply due to increased defense spending, as the following chart illustrates.

Yet mere budget growth does not capture the *qualitative* expansion in government intervention pioneered under President Bush.

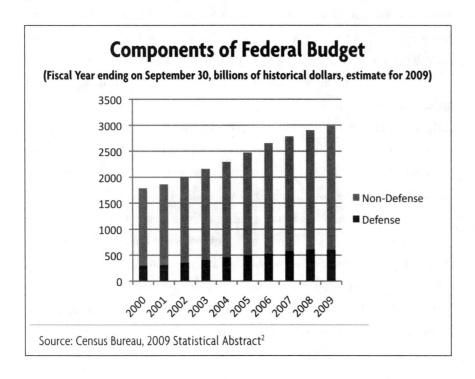

Components of Federal Budget

(Fiscal Year ending on September 30, billions of historical dollars, estimate for 2009)

Source: Census Bureau, 2009 Statistical Abstract[2]

Like Herbert Hoover, George Bush dealt with the economic crisis by providing unprecedented "support" for ailing firms. Through the various novelties designed by Treasury Secretary Henry Paulson and Federal Reserve Chair Ben Bernanke, hundreds of billions of dollars in explicit transfers, and trillions in guarantees, were made from the taxpayers to major financial institutions. By seizing (the press's verb, not mine) Fannie Mae and Freddie Mac, as well as obtaining outright equity positions in commercial banks, the federal government achieved a partial nationalization of the U.S. housing and financial sectors by the time Bush left office. If such moves had been undertaken by a president with a funny name in Bolivia, no one would think of describing them as free market, laissez faire, conservative, or libertarian.

There is another respect in which the Bush presidency was similar to Hoover's. Tragically, the continued escalation of government intervention in 2007 and 2008 was *the reason* the crisis persisted for so long. It had become apparent to both investors and government officials by the summer of 2007 that there would be huge losses on mortgage-related assets, and that heavily exposed financial institutions had to take severe write-downs, possibly throwing some into insolvency. We can imagine what *would have* happened from that point forward, had the Bush team really adhered to laissez-faire as the liberal critics claim. By that time, the damage inflicted by the Fed-fueled boom had already been done; real resources (such as lumber and bricks) had gone towards the construction of too many houses, and those costs were largely sunk. Left to their own devices, investors and fund managers would have assessed the losses, figured out who would bear them, restructured assets among the remaining firms after some went belly up, and then they would have continued with life. The surviving firms would have learned the "lessons of late 2007," they would know that no firm was too big to fail, and they would have taken their junior analysts' warnings more seriously when they pointed out systemic risks in the future. Going into 2008, the financial sector would have been much leaner, perhaps even gaunt, but it would have been wiser and more prudent after the spanking.

But the Bush Administration, under the leadership of Henry Paulson and Ben Bernanke, did not allow this painful yet healthy liquidation. In September 2007 the Fed began its string of unprecedented rate cuts, stopping only when it reached zero. Even at this point, academics discussed other options for "easing," such as Fed purchases of long-dated Treasury securities. Bernanke said repeatedly that the Fed "had more ammunition" with which to help the troubled markets, and that he would continue using his power to help them so long as the situation warranted.

Rather than trusting the classical medicine of liquidation, the Bush Administration held out the promise of a bailout for the biggest firms. The most obvious example came in October 2008 with the $700 billion Troubled Asset Relief Program—a misnomer because rather than buying up troubled assets, Paulson immediately shifted the program into injecting capital into banks to try to "unclog" the credit markets. The TARP money was simply the next logical step in what had been a growing government effort to prop up troubled firms. As early as December 2007 the Fed had already allowed insolvent firms to postpone their bankruptcy, with the Fed providing short-term loans for "toxic" assets.[3]

What happened in the early 1930s was repeated in our time. Because the Bush Administration held out the hope of avoiding hard choices, the firms with the worst balance sheets stalled for time. They strung their investors along with optimistic write-downs, and carried their

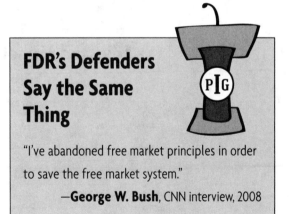

FDR's Defenders Say the Same Thing

"I've abandoned free market principles in order to save the free market system."

—**George W. Bush**, CNN interview, 2008

mortgage-related assets at unrealistic prices on their books. Certain segments of the credit markets froze—though this never posed the threat to small business that Paulson claimed—because of a lack of trust about the banks' assets, something that liquidation (letting the free market work) would have cleared up immediately.

The federal government's emergency measures allowed the troubled firms to limp along, but it came at a steep price, and not only to the taxpayers who have to fund the bailouts, but also to the general health of the economy. Supporting institutions that need to dissolve or restructure themselves does no one any favors in the long run because it ties up labor and capital in unproductive enterprises. From an economist's point of view it is far better to let those businesses liquidate, freeing capital to find better, more profitable uses, which will in turn provide jobs that actually produce real value (producing goods and services that people actually want to buy). Another unintended effect of government bailouts is that it hobbled healthy institutions, which had steered clear of the subprime crisis, because the government lumped all banks and lending institutions into the same TARP boat in order, allegedly, not to erode confidence in the chief offenders.

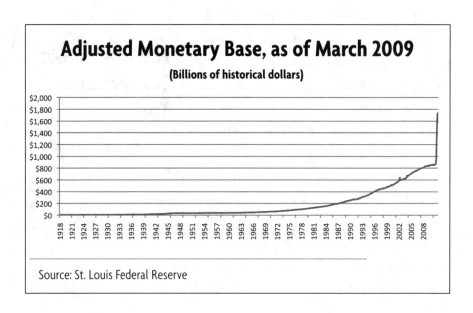

Adjusted Monetary Base, as of March 2009
(Billions of historical dollars)

Source: St. Louis Federal Reserve

All in all, if the Bush Administration had consciously set out to scare away any potential investors in the American financial sector, it could hardly have done a better job. The Securities and Exchange Commission did its part in eroding confidence with its September 2008 (temporary) prohibition on short-sales of stocks—making it *illegal* for speculators to bet on further declines. This was the equivalent of requiring that everyone on Wall Street wear earplugs, thinking this would shut out bad economic news. What it actually did was convince investors that Washington was so panicked that it wouldn't confront reality—or allow investors to confront reality—and let the market set correct prices on assets.

These errors were compounded by the apparently random and haphazard government interventions: allowing the giant investment bank Lehman Brothers to fall one day (it filed for Chapter 11 bankruptcy on September 15, 2008) and then rushing to rescue the insurance giant AIG (in an $85 billion Federal Reserve takeover) the next.

The administration of George W. Bush had always been a big government, big spending one. In its waning months, it took this much farther, interfering with the financial markets as no government had done since the New Deal. Federal Reserve chairman Ben Bernanke, meanwhile, expanded the money supply at a rate that renders the term unprecedented rather inadequate, as you can see by the chart to the left. By any measure, the Bush administration was not laissez faire, not a defender of sound money, and not a friend of limited government. But, like Herbert Hoover, what the Bush administration did do was make laissez-faire economics

Not So Stimulating

"If deficit spending were truly stimulative, then the current [Bush administration] $1.2 trillion budget deficit would already be overheating the economy."

—Brian Riedl

Heritage Foundation fiscal policy analyst, quoted in *The Washington Times*, "Analysts give tax cuts in bill poor grades," by Donald Lambro, February 15, 2009, p A9.

the fall-guy for a stark economic downturn and provide the rationale for liberal, statist policies that could make for a prolonged depression.

Is Barack Obama the New FDR?

The answer could very well be yes—and that would be a disaster. Like FDR, Obama is an ardent supporter of organized labor at a time when wages need to fall in many sectors in order to combat rising unemployment. Environmentalism was not a big issue in FDR's day, but it is a big government crusade for President Obama who will be diverting billions of dollars from his stimulus package into government-selected (rather than market-selected) alternative energy programs. Moreover, the Obama administration intends to use the threat of global warming as a means to strictly regulate the energy markets and how businesses use and pay for energy, putting potentially crushing costs on businesses already squeezed by the economic downturn. But, as Obama said during the campaign, he was content that conventional coal-fired power plants would be driven into bankruptcy through his policies—indeed that was in large part their point.[4]

It was surely no comfort to business leaders to see that President Obama selected a member of the Socialist International's commission on sustainability to fill the (new and informal) post of climate and energy czar.[5] Perhaps even more ominous than the content of the specific policy measures are Obama's candid admissions of his indifference to property rights. As became clear during the campaign, he believes it is the government's job to "spread the wealth" around. He supports hiking the capital gains tax rate for reasons of "fairness," even if such hikes do not bring in more revenue.[6] The whole tenor of the Obama administration is that its ideals are so pure and the economic crisis it confronts is so extraordinary that nothing can be allowed to stand in the way of its policies, which aim not just to restart the economy but to restructure it in the way that liberal Democrats would like it restructured with favored industries offered large government subsidies.

It is hard to imagine that an economic crash caused by Americans living beyond their means—which they were encouraged to do by a reckless Federal Reserve board and a "compassionate conservative" administration busily expanding federal government programs—will be cured by a nearly trillion-dollar "stimulus" package prepared by congressional Democrats eager to dish out the pork to favored constituencies. The stimulus package and related handouts will saddle American taxpayers (and their children) with more government debt than at any time since World War II.

President Obama's stimulus package and other "remedies" will not cure our economic woes any more than the New Deal cured the Great Depression. The real question is whether Barack Obama's New Deal, building on the old one, will finally sink the American economy into the sands.

ACKNOWLEDGEMENTS

would like to thank Harry Crocker of Regnery for suggesting the idea for this book. The need for a volume like this was obvious, but it hadn't occurred to me until reading his email.

Thanks are also in order for Mark Thornton, David Henderson, Robert Wenzel, Joe Salerno, Guido Hülsmann, David Gordon, Thomas Woods, Zach Crossen, Pete Johnson, and others whom I am surely forgetting. I must also thank the members of the Mises Listserv group, who fielded perhaps dozens of questions as I worked on the manuscript. I must also thank my wife Rachael and son Clark, who tolerated my odd sleep schedule as the project neared completion.

NOTES

Chapter 1

1. See Gene Smiley, *Rethinking the Great Depression* (Chicago: Ivan R. Dee, 2002), 4–5.

2. Estimate for March 1933 unemployment rate from Richard K. Vedder and Lowell E. Gallaway, *Out of Work: Unemployment and Government in Twentieth-Century America* (New York: New York University Press, 1997), 77.

3. See http://www.fdic.gov/about/learn/learning/when/1930s.html. (Accessed February 10, 2009.)

4. Quoted in Burton Folsom, Jr., *New Deal or Raw Deal? How FDR's Legacy Has Damaged America* (New York: Threshold Editions, 2008), 2.

Chapter 2

1. Herbert Hoover, *The Memoirs of Herbert Hoover: The Great Depression, 1929-1941* (New York: The Macmillan Company, 1952), 29.

2. Ibid., 30–31.

3. The National Bureau of Economic Research maintains the official dates of U.S. business cycles at this location: http://wwwdev.nber.org/cycles/cyclesmain.html. (Accessed January 14, 2009.) We warn the reader that it is not entirely clear from Hoover's anecdote that Mellon was referring to the 1873–1879 depression, because there were two fairly short contractions (as dated by the N.B.E.R.) from 1865–

1867 and from 1869–1870. These two would obviously fit the "followed the Civil War" description too, but given the explicit description of "the great depression during the seventies" and the severity described by Mellon, we think he is probably referring to the long depression of 1873–1879.

4. According to the N.B.E.R.'s method of dating contractions, the 1870s episode is still the longest on record, but this is because the N.B.E.R. considers the economy to have been in recovery from 1933 until the next contraction hit from 1937–1938. But since the unemployment rate did not fall below 14 percent until the 1940s, we are siding with the man on the street view that "the Depression" lasted throughout the entire 1930s, and hence was much longer than the 1870s depression.

5. Herbert Hoover, *The Memoirs of Herbert Hoover: The Great Depression, 1929-1941* (New York: The Macmillan Company, 1952), 31.

6. Hoover quoted in Murray N. Rothbard, *America's Great Depression*, Fifth Edition (U.S.A.: The Ludwig von Mises Institute, 2008), 190.

7. The early history of Hoover relies heavily on Murray N. Rothbard, *America's Great Depression*, Fifth Edition (U.S.A.: The Ludwig von Mises Institute, 2008), 188–207.

8. Hoover quoted in Murray N. Rothbard, *America's Great Depression*, Fifth Edition (U.S.A.: The Ludwig von Mises Institute, 2008), 205.

9. Herbert Hoover, *The Memoirs of Herbert Hoover: The Great Depression, 1929-1941* (New York: The Macmillan Company, 1952), 25.

10. Quoted in Murray N. Rothbard, *America's Great Depression*, Fifth Edition (U.S.A.: The Ludwig von Mises Institute, 2008), 321.

11. Hoover quoted in Murray N. Rothbard, *America's Great Depression*, Fifth Edition (U.S.A.: The Ludwig von Mises Institute, 2008), 213. The description of Hoover's conferences relies on Rothbard 210–13.

12. Quoted in Murray N. Rothbard, *America's Great Depression*, Fifth Edition (U.S.A.: The Ludwig von Mises Institute, 2008), 268.

13. Richard K. Vedder and Lowell E. Gallaway, *Out of Work: Unemployment and Government in Twentieth-Century America* (New York: New York University Press, 1997), 81.

14. Ibid., 57.

15. Ibid., 77. We note that the monthly figures are based on Vedder and Gallaway's model estimates, since monthly unemployment data was not recorded this early in U.S history.

16. Burton Folsom, Jr., *New Deal or Raw Deal? How FDR's Legacy Has Damaged America* (New York: Threshold Editions, 2008), 31.

17. Ibid.

18. Paul Krugman, "Fifty Herbert Hoovers," *New York Times*, December 29, 2008, page A25, available at: http://www.nytimes.com/2008/12/29/opinion/29krugman.html?partner=permalink&exprod=permalink . (Accessed January 16, 2009.)

19.Bicentennial Edition: Historical Statistics of the United States, From Colonial Times to 1970, Series Y 335-338, available at: http://www2.census.gov/prod2/statcomp/documents/CT1970p2-12.pdf (Accessed January 17, 2009.)

20. Budget table adapted from The American Presidency Project, available at: http://www.presidency.ucsb.edu/data/budget.php . (Accessed January 17, 2009.)

21. See the Tax Foundation, "U.S. Federal Income Tax Rates History, 1913-2009," available at: http://taxfoundation.org/taxdata/show/151.html.

22. Bicentennial Edition: Historical Statistics of the United States, From Colonial Times to 1970, Series Y 335-338, available at: http://www2.census.gov/prod2/statcomp/documents/CT1970p2-12.pdf. (Accessed January 17, 2009.)

23. Ibid.

24. See for example Paul Krugman, "Deficits and the Future," *New York Times*, December 1, 2008, page A29, available at: http://www.nytimes.com/2008/12/01/opinion/01krugman.html?_r=1&partner=rssnyt&emc=rss. (Accessed on January 17, 2009.)

25. Murray N. Rothbard, *America's Great Depression*, Fifth Edition (U.S.A.: The Ludwig von Mises Institute, 2008), 286–87.

26. Historical tax rates available at: http://taxfoundation.org/taxdata/show/151.html. (Accessed February 2, 2009.)

27. Murray N. Rothbard, *America's Great Depression*, Fifth Edition (U.S.A.: The Ludwig von Mises Institute, 2008), 227 and 229.

28. Ibid., 232.

29. This section is drawn from Murray N. Rothbard, *America's Great Depression*, Fifth Edition (U.S.A.: The Ludwig von Mises Institute, 2008), 216–17.

30. Murray N. Rothbard, *America's Great Depression*, Fifth Edition (U.S.A.: The Ludwig von Mises Institute, 2008), 239.

31. Ibid., 295.

32. Ibid., 299.

33. Burton Folsom, Jr., *New Deal or Raw Deal? How FDR's Legacy Has Damaged America* (New York: Threshold Editions, 2008), 39.

34. For more on this point, see Jonah Goldberg, *Liberal Fascism: The Secret History of the Left, from Mussolini to the Politics of Meaning* (New York: Doubleday, 2008).

35. Herbert Hoover, *The Memoirs of Herbert Hoover: The Great Depression, 1929-1941* (New York: The Macmillan Company, 1952), 17.

36. Ibid., 24–25.

Chapter 3

1. Ben Bernanke's remarks available at: http://www.federalreserve.gov/BOARDDOCS/SPEECHES/2002/20021108/default.htm. (Accessed January 20, 2009.)

2. Bank reserve data maintained by the St. Louis Fed at: http://research.stlouisfed.org/fred2/categories/123. (Accessed February 2, 2009.)

3. Milton Friedman, *Free to Choose: A Personal Statement* (New York: Harcourt Books, 1990), 79–80.

4. Jim Powell, *FDR's Folly: How Roosevelt and His New Deal Prolonged the Great Depression* (New York: Three Rivers Press, 2003), 29–30.

5. Peter Bernstein, from the Introduction to Milton Friedman and Anna Schwartz, *The Great Contraction: 1929-1933* (Princeton: Princeton University Press, 2008 [1963]), xxx.

6. Annual deflation figures calculated as the January-over-January changes in monthly CPI, available at the St. Louis Fed: http://research. stlouisfed.org/fred2/series/CPIAUCNS?cid=9.

7. Gene Smiley, *Rethinking the Great Depression* (Chicago: Ivan R. Dee, 2002), 6.

8. Murray Rothbard, *A History of Money and Banking in the United States: The Colonial Era to World War II* (Auburn, AL: The Ludwig von Mises Institute, 2002), 103.

9. Ibid.

10. See Ronald McKinnon, "Bagehot's Lessons for the Fed," *Wall Street Journal*, April 25, 2008, page A15, available at: http://online.wsj.com/article/SB120908336730343529.html. (Accessed January 23, 2009.)

11. Lionel Robbins, *The Great Depression* (Auburn, AL: The Ludwig von Mises Institute, 2007 [1934]), 73.

12. Historical NY Fed discount rate data available at: http://fraser.stlouis-fed.org/publications/bms/issue/61/download/132/section12.pdf. (Accessed February 1, 2009.)

13. Economists Thomas E. Hall and J. David Ferguson, quoted in Jim Powell, *FDR's Folly: How Roosevelt and His New Deal Prolonged the Great Depression* (New York: Three Rivers Press, 2003), 37.

Chapter 4

1. Gene Smiley, *Rethinking the Great Depression* (Chicago: Ivan R. Dee, 2002), 4.

2. Gene Smiley, *Rethinking the Great Depression* (Chicago: Ivan R. Dee, 2002), 5-6.

3. Data refer to fiscal years. Bicentennial Edition: Historical Statistics of the United States, From Colonial Times to 1970, Series Y 335-338, available at: http://www2.census.gov/prod2/statcomp/documents/CT1970p2-12.pdf (Accessed January 19, 2009.)

4. Andrew Mellon quoted in http://en.wikipedia.org/wiki/Andrew_Mellon. (Accessed January 19, 2009.)

5. John Kenneth Galbraith, *The Great Crash*, 1929 (Boston: Mariner Books, 1997).

6. Quoted in Lionel Robbins, *The Great Depression* (Auburn, AL: The Ludwig von Mises Institute, 2007 [1934]), 53.

7. Strictly speaking, the term *trade deficit* refers narrowly to an imbalance in goods and services traded between countries. In the text we are actually referring to an overall balance of payments deficit in which all American items for sale, including financial assets such as government bonds and corporate stock, do not attract enough British buyers to offset the desired American purchases of British trade and assets. It is thus a balance of payments deficit, not the popular "trade deficit," that would cause the dollar to depreciate against the pound. If the British wanted to invest more in American stocks and bonds than Americans wanted to invest in British assets, then this capital account surplus could finance a trade deficit, with no impact on the dollar/pound exchange rate of $4.86. In fact, this is exactly what happened for most of the late 1800s, as the rapidly industrializing and relatively laissez-faire United States was a magnet for investors the world over. See Gene Smiley, Rethinking the Great Depression (Chicago: Ivan R. Dee, 2002), 46.

8. Murray Rothbard, *What Has Government Done to Our Money?* (Auburn, AL: The Ludwig von Mises Institute, 2008), 91-92.

9. Historical gold prices from this site: http://www.zaverat.com/d_gold-pricerecord.php. (Accessed January 28, 2009.)

Chapter 5

1. Historical unemployment rates obtained from: http://www.bls.gov/opub/cwc/cm20030124ar03p1.htm. (Accessed January 30, 2009.)

2. Quoted in David Sirota, "Did you hear FDR prolonged the Great Depression?" Slate, January 2, 2009, available at: http://www.salon.com/opinion/feature/2009/01/02/sirota_fdr_depression/index.html. (Accessed January 31, 2009.)

3. Real GDP data available from the St. Louis Fed at: http://research.stlouisfed.org/fred2/data/GDPCA.txt. (Accessed January 31, 2009.)

4. Harold L. Cole and Lee E. Ohanian, "New Deal Policies and the Persistence of the Great Depression: A General Equilibrium Analysis," UCLA Economics Department Research Memo, February 2003, available at: http://hlcole.bol.ucla.edu/NewDealucla.pdf. (Accessed January 28, 2009.)

5. Quoted in Burton Folsom, Jr., *New Deal or Raw Deal? How FDR's Legacy Has Damaged America* (New York: Threshold Editions, 2008), 12.

6. U.S. unemployment rates from: http://www.bls.gov/opub/cwc/cm20030124ar03p1.htm. Canadian unemployment data computed from workforce data at: http://www.statcan.gc.ca/cgi-bin/af-fdr.cgi?l=eng&loc=D124_133-eng.csv. (Accessed January 31, 2009.)

7. Quoted in Robert Higgs, *Depression, War, and Cold War* (New York: Oxford University Press, 2006), 12–13.

8. See the BLS series on CPI at: http://research.stlouisfed.org/fred2/data/CPIAUCNS.txt. (Accessed January 31, 2009.)

9. Harold L. Cole and Lee E. Ohanian, "New Deal Policies and the Persistence of the Great Depression: A General Equilibrium Analysis," UCLA Economics Department Research Memo, February 2003, available at: http://hlcole.bol.ucla.edu/NewDealucla.pdf, 3–4.

10. Ibid., 4.

11. Ibid., 6.

12. Ibid., 43, 45.

13. Robert Higgs, *Depression, War, and Cold War* (New York: Oxford University Press, 2006), 7.

14. Garet Garrett, ed. Bruce Ramsey, *Salvos Against the New Deal: Selections from the Saturday Evening Post* 1933-1940 (U.S.A.: Caxton Press, 2002), 216–17.

15. See the November 2008 video of Will and Krugman at: http://www.youtube.com/watch?v=3yAyQV8gOjo. (Accessed January 31, 2009.)

16. The original paper was Robert Higgs, "Regime Uncertainty: Why the Great Depression Lasted So Long and Why Prosperity Resumed after the War," The Independent Review, Vol. 1, No. 4, Spring 1997. The paper is reprinted as chapter 1 in Robert Higgs, *Depression, War, and Cold War* (New York: Oxford University Press, 2006).

17. Robert Higgs, *Depression, War, and Cold War* (New York: Oxford University Press, 2006), 5.

18. For a summary of the literature, see Lawrence McQuillan and Robert P. Murphy, "The Sizzle of Economic Freedom" (Pacific Research Institute, 2009), available at: http://pacificresearch.org/docLib/20090106_Economic_Sizzle.pdf. (Accessed January 31, 2009.)

19. Burton Folsom, Jr., *New Deal or Raw Deal? How FDR's Legacy Has Damaged America* (New York: Threshold Editions, 2008), 103.

20. Ibid., 106.

21. Ibid., 110.

22. Robert Higgs, *Depression, War, and Cold War* (New York: Oxford University Press, 2006), 9.

23. Ibid., 18.

24. Grant sought a third term in 1880 after taking four years off, but lost the Republican nomination to Garfield.

25. Quoted in Burton Folsom, Jr., *New Deal or Raw Deal? How FDR's Legacy Has Damaged America* (New York: Threshold Editions, 2008), 136.

26. Quoted in Burton Folsom, Jr., *New Deal or Raw Deal? How FDR's Legacy Has Damaged America* (New York: Threshold Editions, 2008), 137.

27. Ibid., 25.

Chapter 6

1. Entry for "March 5, 1933: Roosevelt Declares Bank Holiday" at: http://www.history.com/this-day-in-history.do?action=Article&id=5755. (Accessed February 1, 2009.)

2. See for example George Selgin, "Should We Let Banks Create Money?" *The Independent Review*, vol. V, No. 1, Summer 2000, available at: http://www.independent.org/pdf/tir/tir_05_1_selgin.pdf. (Accessed February 1, 2009.)

3. Quoted in Jim Powell, *FDR's Folly: How Roosevelt and His New Deal Prolonged the Great Depression* (New York: Three Rivers Press, 2003), 55.

4. Mary Ann Milbourn, "IndyMac reopens as worried customers check on their accounts," *Orange County Register*, July 14, 2008, available at: http://www.ocregister.com/articles/bank-people-time-2093028-federal-indymac. (Accessed February 1, 2009.)

5. Jim Powell, *FDR's Folly: How Roosevelt and His New Deal Prolonged the Great Depression* (New York: Three Rivers Press, 2003), 57.

6. Economist George Benston, quoted in Jim Powell, *FDR's Folly: How Roosevelt and His New Deal Prolonged the Great Depression* (New York: Three Rivers Press, 2003), 62.

7. Jim Powell, *FDR's Folly: How Roosevelt and His New Deal Prolonged the Great Depression* (New York: Three Rivers Press, 2003), 31.

8. Ibid., 32.

9. Ibid., 33.

10. Gene Smiley, *Rethinking the Great Depression* (Chicago: Ivan R. Dee, 2002), 77.

11. Jim Powell, *FDR's Folly: How Roosevelt and His New Deal Prolonged the Great Depression* (New York: Three Rivers Press, 2003), 67.

12. Ibid., 74.

13. Burton Folsom, Jr., *New Deal or Raw Deal? How FDR's Legacy Has Damaged America* (New York: Threshold Editions, 2008), 105.

14. Ibid., 55.

15. Pharis quotations from Burton Folsom, Jr., *New Deal or Raw Deal? How FDR's Legacy Has Damaged America* (New York: Threshold Editions, 2008), 50–51.

16. Amity Shlaes, *The Forgotten Man: A New History of the Great Depression* (New York: HarperCollins, 2007), 217.

17. Ibid., 224.

18. Ibid., 241.

19. Quoted at: http://robaroundbooks.com/2008/09/grapes-of-wrath-after-thoughts/. (Accessed February 2, 2009.)

20. Jim Powell, *FDR's Folly: How Roosevelt and His New Deal Prolonged the Great Depression* (New York: Three Rivers Press, 2003), 134–136.

21. Ibid., 134.

22. Ibid., 184.

23. See http://www.cbo.gov/ftpdocs/96xx/doc9649/08-20-SocialSecurityUpdate.pdf. (Accessed February 2, 2009.)

24. Burton Folsom, Jr., *New Deal or Raw Deal? How FDR's Legacy Has Damaged America* (New York: Threshold Editions, 2008), 181.

25. Ibid.

26. Ibid., 188–189.

27. Ibid., 182.

28. Ibid., 70.

Chapter 7

1. Henry Hazlitt, *Economics In One Lesson* (New York: Crown Publishers, Inc., 1979), 25–26.

2. Ibid., 26.

3. Bob Higgs' work in this area dates back to a 1992 peer-reviewed article in *The Journal of Economic History*, and is collected in Robert Higgs, *Depression, War, and Cold War: Studies in Political Economy* (New York: Oxford University Press, 2006).

4. Robert Higgs, *Depression, War, and Cold War* (New York: Oxford University Press, 2006), 62–63.

5. Ibid., 4.

6. In 1943 the U.S. federal budget deficit (i.e. not expenditures) was an astounding 30.3% of GDP; by 1945 it had fallen to 21.5%, itself a shocking number. See http://www.presidency.ucsb.edu/data/budget.php. (Accessed January 10, 2009.)

7. See the entry on "World War II" at: http://www.u-s-history.com/pages/h1661.html. (Accessed January 9, 2009.)

8. See the entry on "World War II" at: http://www.u-s-history.com/pages/h1661.html. (Accessed January 9, 2009.)

9. See the entry on "Lend-Lease" at: http://en.wikipedia.org/wiki/Lend-Lease#Repayment. (Accessed January 9, 2009.) Even though the British

formally discharged their Lend-Lease debt, they had initially received an enormous discount on the retained goods.

10. Ibid., 18–19.

11. Ibid., 19.

Chapter 8

1. Jonathan McCarthy and Richard W. Peach, "Is There a 'Bubble' in the Housing Market Now?" New York Federal Reserve Research Paper, 2005, available at: http://www.newyorkfed.org/research/economists/mccarthy/athens_bubble_paper.pdf. (Accessed January 28, 2009.)

2. Federal budget data available at: http://www.census.gov/compendia/statab/cats/federal_govt_finances_empl oyment/federal_budgetreceipts_outlays_and_debt.html. (Accessed January 28, 2009.)

3. For a timeline of the financial crisis and the government's response, see the St. Louis Fed's summary here: http://www.stlouisfed.org/timeline/pdf/CrisisTimeline.pdf. (Accessed January 29, 2009.)

4. Obama interview with *San Francisco Chronicle*, detailed at: http://newsbusters.org/blogs/p-j-gladnick/2008/11/02/hidden-audio-obama-tells-sf-chronicle-he-will-bankrupt-coal-industry. (Accessed January 30, 2009.) . "An auction on the cap and trade system, which means that every unit of carbon or greenhouse gases that was emitted would be charged to the polluter. That will create a market in which whatever technologies are out there that are being presented, whatever power plants that are being built that they would have to meet the rigors of that market and the ratcheted down caps that are placed, imposed every year. So if somebody wants to build a coal powered plant, they can. It's just that it will bankrupt them because they are going to be charged a huge sum."—Barack Obama, January 2008

5. On Carol Browner's connection to the Socialist International, see http://consultingbyrpm.com/blog/2009/01/obama-nominates-socialist.html. (Accessed January 30, 2009.)

6. On Obama's discussion of the capital gains tax, see the video at: http://www.youtube.com/watch?v=WpSDBu35K-8. (Accessed January 30, 2009.)

INDEX